All You Need Is What You Have

All You Need Is What You Have

Using Your Five Senses Creatively to Move through Grief

VALERIE MOORE-ALTAVILLA, LCSW

Hanford Mead Publishers, Inc.
Santa Cruz, California USA

FIRST EDITION

ISBN No. 10: 1-59275-044-3

ISBN No. 13: 978-1-59275-044-3

Manufactured in the United States of America (alk. paper)

10 9 8 7 6 5 4 3 2 1

This edition is printed on acid-free paper that meets the American National Standards Institute Z39.48 Standard.

Library of Congress Cataloging-in-Publication Data

Names: Moore-Altavilla, Valerie, 1976- author.
Title: All you need is what you have : using your five senses creatively to
   move through grief / Valerie Moore-Altavilla, LCSW.
Description: First edition. | Santa Cruz, California : Hanford Mead
   Publishers, Inc., [2020] | Includes bibliographical references. |
   Summary: "Valerie Moore-Altavilla, LCSW, instinctively used the
   expressive arts to metabolize grief from the multiple losses of her
   loved ones that began when she was 9. Now, professionally trained as a
   social worker, in the career for which life was already preparing her,
   she shares in this book what she has learned about how to grieve.
   Valerie trusts each person to know how to proceed on their individual
   journey. She guides the reader on how to take stock of their strengths
   as well as their losses and how to soothe themselves. She suggests easy
   projects to use in moving along the grieving path through all its
   memories, thoughts, and sensations. 58 full-color graphics"-- Provided
   by publisher.
Identifiers: LCCN 2020034382 (print) | LCCN 2020034383 (ebook) | ISBN
   9781592750443 (paperback) | ISBN 9781592750467 (ebook)
Subjects: LCSH: Grief. | Loss (Psychology) | Bereavement.
Classification: LCC BF575.G7 M653 2020 (print) | LCC BF575.G7 (ebook) |
   DDC 155.9/37--dc23
LC record available at https://lccn.loc.gov/2020034382
LC ebook record available at https://lccn.loc.gov/2020034383

Contents

Acknowledgments

My good friend and former colleague Mary Ransom gave me the encouragement from which stemmed the idea to put my thoughts and ideas into a book format. Mary has been so supportive and encouraging along the way, with the nudges needed to keep at it with this book.

I also want to thank all of those beautiful friends who took the time to read, re-read, and critique my book, and who tried out the exercises. Those include Mary Ransom, Connie Moore, Cathy McNease, and Virginia Moreno. A big thank you to my husband Brad who was patient and supportive throughout my process with this book. And I have such gratitude for my parents who have always believed in me and given me the encouragement I have needed along the way in life. I couldn't begin to list all of the loving supports in my life here, but you know who you are and I am very grateful. I thank Kylea Taylor, my publisher through Hanford Mead, who has been instrumental in this whole process.

I send a special thank you to my good friends Paul Dunkley and Harmony Agh who have generously allowed me to use their beautiful captivating images to further enhance my book.

Foreword

I am excited to write this foreword because, as an experienced grief counselor, I am aware that talk therapy is sometimes not enough. Some people are not able to get in touch with their emotions through words. Some people get stuck in the various phases of their grief journey. The way *through* the difficult journey of loss may be found using the exercises in this simple yet profound book.

I believe in the "buffet approach" to therapy. You take a little of this and a little of that. The more you take, in terms of varied modalities of treatment, the healthier your overall healing will be.

Expressive arts is a modality you don't want to leave out. The more you integrate your losses using all your senses and both sides of your brain, the healthier you will be. Reading a book or going to talk therapy uses one side of the brain. But using the other side of your brain and incorporating your senses helps complete—or at least complements—the steps along the grief journey.

I worked with Valerie during our years at Hospice of Santa Barbara. We also co-facilitated a seminar about grief. She is humble and reserved, kind and authentic. From what she has learned on her own journey, Valerie knows the importance of creating for healing. Sharing this passion with others is her mission.

Sometimes Valerie was called upon to lead Art Therapy exercises during our hour-long staff meetings. Those of us who could barely draw stick figures would groan in dismay. But she would gently give us instructions, turn on soft music, and say, "Remember it's the *process*, not the product."

At the hour's end, we would feel so surprised about the feeling behind the project. It truly is the *process* of the creation. Without effort one is taken to a different place of understanding, a deeper level of healing. The shallow breath gives way to a fuller one.

Imagine having more than an hour to explore what you weren't aware you had. What you have is within you—your senses. This book guides you there in a most personal and loving way. If you have suffered a loss, you need to read this book.

– Mary Ransom, Author of *Courage Road: A Guide from Grief to Hope*

Preface

My personal odyssey with grief started at a relatively young age when I lost my grandmother. I had been intimately involved in her end-of-life care, so her loss and my grief was significant. Through the years I have journeyed through several more significant losses. Each loss has re-shaped my belief system; redefining who I am and what life means. Through these profound losses, I have gained a greater appreciation for life. I recognize the small things more often, and I take less for granted. I love in a deeper and stronger way. The combination of my personal losses and my professional experiences have strengthened me in ways I could never have imagined.

Anderson Cooper interviewed Steven Colbert about his grief journey since the loss of his father and two of his brothers in a plane crash when he was ten years old. Anderson Cooper also experienced the loss of his father at age ten. At one point in the interview, Steven Colbert said that the fullness of humanity is to feel suffering and be grateful for the things we wished didn't happen because, "they give the gift of being able to connect with others in their suffering." I, too, feel that this suffering has given me a gift, the gift to be able to journey with others on their path to healing through grief.

Both of my parents were in the helping professions. My father was a psychologist. My mother was a school counselor. So, perhaps I was destined to be in a helping profession as well. I have degrees in both Psychology and Social work. Early in my career I worked in mental health and foster care. The thing is, as mortal beings, we will all experience grief at some point. Nobody escapes death or the loss of loved ones. I discovered that no matter in what area of social work I found myself, grief was at its core. Many people I have worked with have had unresolved grief issues that blocked their healing. To love and lose, or not to love at all? Well, we certainly hurt and grieve because we love. However, if we don't love, there can be no emotion or feeling.

From a relatively young age, without knowing about or calling it "art therapy," I utilized expressive arts as a way to heal from my own losses. When my brother

Shawn came to live with me in my early 20's after a temporarily successful rehabil-itation program, I gave him some paper, paints, and had him go into a room and just paint it out. Then I sat with him, listened, and helped him make sense of what came out on the paper. It was a beautiful process and experience. I think it was at this point I knew this tool needed to be a part of my professional practice. It took a few years for my path in art therapy to become a reality.

My ultimate calling to do grief work didn't fully become consciously apparent until I completed the 18-month post-masters art therapy program in San Diego at UCSD in 2007. As a requirement of this program, I was placed in an internship, which happened to be in a hospice setting. During my internship at San Diego Hospice and Palliative Care, I completed extensive training, which included the experience of writing my own obituary. I had just turned 30, was newly divorced and had moved to a new state to start the next chapter of my life. During this training, I connected to the various "stages" of grief as related to my recent divorce and to my mother's stage 3 uterine cancer diagnosed during this same time (she did survive). I was grieving many non-death loss issues and feeling possible anticipatory grief. I learned much about myself and the grief process. I learned the importance of having information and knowledge and how to share it with others in my professional work.

The internship at hospice intensified my belief that art therapy and grief work was my true calling. I remember poignantly the words an end-of-life client said to me. She said, "Why is everyone around here wearing black? I am the one dying here. Wear some color!" She had been a professional artist in her earlier years. She shared she believed we are born into this world with no attachments. However, before we leave the world, we have established them. She elaborated that one of the harder parts of her end-of-life journey was the "letting go" part. She was so vibrant and full of life even in her last days. I was so moved by her that I made a magazine collage in response to her spirit and what she shared with me about her life and gave it to her. Later, I made one of my own to process the experience.

I love to journey with people of all ages in all stages of life. Each person takes this journey in their own unique way. I love the act of presence; to just sit with someone, to listen, to guide, to provide education on the grief process, to help them to discover new insights. Many gifts can emerge amidst the weight of grief. Witnessing the hope and transformations that time and healing provide is so profound and beautiful. What an honor for me to be a part of someone else's journey, if even for a moment. My hope with this book is to help provide tools to as many people as I can, to help their journey of grief be filled with hope and light.

Introduction

"Wherever you are is where you are supposed to be."
~ Valerie Moore-Altavilla

You've opened this book and are a little curious to see if there are some appealing ways to take care of yourself and work through your loss(es). That's great. Take a little time. Read a little, look through the pictures, scan the exercises.

Grief is what many might call an uninvited visitor who comes to stay for a while. So, maybe we can make friends with this visitor? Maybe even discover some of the hidden gifts it might have for us? You will find choices in this book and can choose the ways through grief that feel right to you.

I invite you to let go of any expectations you might have, and just really listen to yourself to hear what you need in any given moment. Let the book, with me as your guide, take you into whatever direction it leads. Wherever you are is where you are supposed to be! Just go with it! Try to just trust the process, and the unknowns that will unfold in time. There is no right or wrong way to do this thing called grief.

All humans encounter grief at some point in life. The loss of a loved one, loss of a job, loss of relationship, the loss of a pet, or loss of youth creates a void and grief. Often not just once, but many times, pain and loss cross our paths.

Soul/Body

Along this path of pain, suffering and grief, there is also opportunity for growth and transformation. The key is to allow ourselves to process, to work through these feelings, invite insight, and shed light on the pain.

The creative exercises presented in this book have been utilized by me and by those with whom I've worked as a therapist. This book of creative healing after loss was inspired by both personal and professional journeys in the realm of death and dying. They have proven to be useful, meaningful and healing. Time and time again, after doing one of the healing exercises in this book, participants have talked about some profound insight, how a process helped them get unstuck, how what came up was something they didn't even know was under the surface, something needing some attention and healing. They exclaim about how what felt totally impossible was actually doable.

Art therapy has been my saving grace in times when my mind just took over with thoughts like, "I can't handle this loss," "I'll never survive," "I will just always be an anxious mess." Through trial and error, I stumbled onto creating and writing as a means of working through emotions and feelings held in my body. I was able to get out of my head and step into my body, where I could listen to my gut. This is what really helped me begin to heal my whole self. Every time I did a magazine collage or scribble drawing (which I explain later), there was a big release and new insight. Each time a layer peeled off, it helped me get to the core.

Healing begins with bringing awareness to the role our bodily organs and the senses (vision, hearing, touch, smell and taste) play in our healing process. Listening to the body is an integral part of understanding the mind. We often hear the term "gut feeling." This is the sensation we feel, originating in the stomach that is an unconscious reaction to a situation or to our surroundings. Often this "gut feeling" is dismissed and the mind takes over. If we instead tune into this body response or "gut feeling," listen to the message and trust it, the body and mind begin to work together for true, lasting healing, not just temporary relief.

As you read, you will find a variety of exercises to explore that will help you tune into your body and listen to that "gut" feeling. Though these exercises are in a certain order in the book, there is no particular order for doing them. Just start with something that sounds interesting.

———————————————

My experience with loss and grief began at a relatively young age. I was 11 years old when my maternal grandmother was diagnosed with colon cancer and chose not to be treated. She moved in with my family during her end of life. Family members would take turns sleeping on the couch outside her room at night.

I remember my grandmother insisting on paying me $1 each day to help her with medications and other needs. Although my grandmother was in severe pain, she always brushed it off, selflessly wanting me to be a kid and play outside. I often sat in her room holding her hand. I did this more often during her last days when she was no longer in a conscious state. One sunny afternoon, as I was just holding her hand and talking to her (though I do not remember the words I said) she took her last breath. I alerted my mother and father who confirmed my grandmother had died.

Though 30 years have passed, I remember that poignant moment as if it were yesterday. One does not ever "get over" the loss of a loved one. We just learn ways to carry on a happy and healthy life, while creating a special place for them in our heart.

In 2015, my brother Shawn died. He had been estranged from the family for over 12 years. No one knew for a long time if he were dead or alive. However, through random circumstances we did reconnect with him just a year before he died. At this time, he was in poor health due to a long history of substance abuse. Shawn had not accepted his rapidly declining health and was in denial that the end of his life was so near. Everybody else was experiencing the same denial despite obvious signs and the doctor's prognosis. This is actually a quite common phenomenon. Sometimes what the mind knows, the heart doesn't want to believe.

Shawn's long-term girlfriend (soulmate) told us that he was on life support. His only hope was an innovative heart surgery. As the doctors opened his heart cavity the condition was far worse than expected and the final hope was gone. Although family members flew in from various states, I was the only family member to make it to his bedside in time to say goodbye. As the heart monitor flat-lined, I lovingly spoke as many words as I could while rubbing his forehead. The nurse said, "He's gone." A tear rolled down the side of his face and I stood silently by him.

My sense was that his spirit was departing, leaving a final goodbye tear.

I had grieved for years the unknowns, the "unfinished business" of the loss of my brother before his actual death. I would ask myself questions. Is he homeless? Did he die? If he did die, would I even know it? During these years I processed my loss through the creative exercises I suggest to you in this book. Everyone experiences loss. Everyone grieves. Everyone grieves differently, but these exercises are universal and support healing for all types of loss.

Grief can be a roller coaster ride through a complicated and sticky mess of emotions and feelings. There is no right or wrong way to grieve and everyone experiences different feelings and emotions based on a variety of circumstances, such as the type of relationship with the loved one, whether it was a sudden or expected loss, or if we have worked through previous losses at the time a new loss occurs.

In between losing my grandmother and my brother, I experienced other profound losses very close to my heart and soul that did not have adequate closure, such as the loss of another brother to suicide, a perinatal loss at 18 weeks of pregnancy, and others. You, too, may also have not just one loss, but other unfinished losses you are dealing with now.

Boy smiling

The healing process in this book is designed with tools and methods of practice to create this powerful connection between mind and body, a process to heal the whole self. I've started the book with an introduction to grief before getting into the heart of the healing through creative exercises.

The art created in these exercises is for the process of healing. A *process* is different from a *product* or a final *outcome*.

We can find an example by looking through the eyes of a child for just a moment. We adults can learn from children. I recently was watching a three-year-old paint. I was completely fascinated and entranced by the experience. He was painting, mixing different colors, not caring if it got muddy. He was having so much fun, just free and happy. As he painted, he would talk about what he was painting. "I'm painting lamp posts!" To someone observing, it might have looked like a muddy mess, but to him, it was his soul–visual images from his mind being transferred onto the paper. We can learn from this experience to unwind and be free, not caring about judgment from ourselves or others. We can learn to let the inner critic go and simply experience.

Boy Painting

Most people come to my Healing Arts groups and workshops with some hesitation or resistant feeling that their "artistic" skills will take them no further than a stick figure. However, I found that it's the "professional artist" who sometimes finds this art most challenging. When one makes art for a living, they are often creating a piece of work for a desired result or product. It is hard to let go of this focus on outcome and just create spontaneously, expressing what is coming from the heart and soul.

We are all artists in some way. In art therapy, the end goal is not to create an aesthetically pleasing piece of art. It is more about getting images from your mind and feelings (nonverbal) out of your head and onto paper. This process is an expression of you. It's not about making "good" art! It's about letting go of what other people think and just being free like the child we all once were and still are. That inner child is a part of us all, but for some it is hidden in a deep place within and just needs the opportunity and permission to reemerge. Art therapy is about getting out of the head; the left side of the brain, the mind that is chatting away, and getting into the body and the right side of the brain that is nonverbal, our feelings and memories. The mind is good at playing tricks, talking us into or out of things, but the body is good at telling us what is truly going on.

Later in the book I give examples of great beginner exercises to help get into this creative space and build more confidence in self and trusting the process.

List of helpful materials:

Here is a suggestion of supplies that might be helpful to have on hand for a richer experience:

- Journal / Paper
- Writing utensils (pen, pencil)
- Colored pencils
- Markers / Sharpies
- Oil pastels
- Acrylic paints
- Glue
- Scissors
- Magazines
- Photos

In the world of art therapy, we use a different medium depending on our particular need in the moment. First, a *medium* refers to the type of materials one uses when creating. You could use pencil, crayon, ink, chalk pastel, oil pastel, acrylic paint, oil paint, watercolor. If you were overwhelmed with emotion, and wanted to contain it, then you could use a dry medium such as pencil or colored pencil. If you were feeling stuck and needing to have a release of emotion, then using a more fluid medium such as paints might help.

CHAPTER 1

What Is Grief?

We are formed by grieving like sea glass in the ocean.
We are weathered by nature, constantly being re-shaped
and re-worked in a process of transformation.

Grief is all of the thoughts and feelings one experiences when impacted by a loss. In this book I am mainly addressing the grief that comes when we lose a significant other through death, but grief comes from all types of non-death losses too, such as divorce, empty nest when children have left home, a move to a new town, disability, addiction, loss of a job, a pandemic, or natural disasters destroying homes and communities.

This book will introduce ways to augment talk therapy to process and work through these feelings. Healing can happen through creating and letting go of expectations. Often there just aren't words to say to express a feeling. How often has someone asked how you are feeling, and you are at a loss as to how to respond?

There is a great value to talk therapy and survivor's groups. There is a camaraderie that takes place in talk groups, a connection that is made with others who are journeying through a similar loss, such as loss of a child, spouse, parent, sibling, loved one to suicide, a pet, and they learn ways to "survive," ways to cope, ways to navigate through this "new" way of living life with others who have similar challenges and experiences.

Groups have been proven to be an effective and profound support to people of all ages who have experienced a significant loss including children/teens. I have the opportunity to work with children/teens in a group setting providing grief support. Often in grief support groups for children/teens, I incorporate art, music, and writing exercises as a part of the experience. And in fact, children, especially aged 12 and younger, naturally tend to express feelings and behaviors through art and play. In group settings, just as with adults, children/teens make a profound connection with one another. It is so helpful for children/teens to have a safe place to talk about their loss, especially in a time in their development when they want to feel normal, to just fit in, and not feel different than their peers.

Support groups give people permission to grieve openly, to share their story and hear others' stories. Each type of group (verbal sharing, expressive arts, and a combination of both) has its place and importance. For the purpose of this book, I am just providing some additional tools and ways for you to work through your life and loss independently through expressive arts.

What is "normal" when grieving? The answer is "anything and everything," from feeling nothing (numb) to feeling angry, or sad and happy at the same time. There is no "right" way to grieve. It is a uniquely individual process for each person. When taking this journey, it is important to check in with yourself at various times and identify what is coming up for you as it is ever changing like the motion of the ocean. We are formed by grieving like sea glass in the ocean. We are weathered by nature, constantly being re-shaped and re-worked in a process of transformation. As hard as it may be at times, if you get stuck in a painful feeling, just remember that the feeling will pass, it will morph and change because everything changes. You can count on this. It is ok to feel whatever is coming up for you. As Allan Lokos quoted in his book *Pocket Peace: Effective Practices for Enlightened living,* "Don't believe everything you think. Thoughts are just that–thoughts." (2010).

It's important to remember that you are never alone in grief, though at times it will feel that way. Each person has their own journey and story, but the world is full of people who are grieving in some way. They're feeling numb, confused, sad, angry, or any other number of feelings associated with profound loss.

It is good to remember that there are more people actively grieving than will admit to it. Sometimes people expect that after six months or a year has passed, the grieving should be over. There is an expectation that it is time to move on. With that cultural message, many people keep these feelings inside, unexposed to the world as much as possible for fear of being judged in some way. But the truth is we may not get to the heart of the grief until a year or two down the road, or even longer. The length of grieving after the loss of a loved one depends on so many circumstances and layers. One never "gets over" such a profound loss; we just learn how to live a new "normal," as life is forever changed. Our relationship with the person we have lost is redefined. There is still a relationship, just not the physical one we once knew.

Mark Liebenow, an independent writer wrote a beautiful blog on "metabolizing grief," a term initially coined by author Martín Prechtel. Liebenow discusses the very organic nature of grief and describes that just as the body metabolizes food and converts it into energy, so the heart metabolizes grief. "Today's grief is today's grief. Make no judgment about it. It is what it is. Work with it." (cited in Liebenow, 2018, para. 10).

Liebenow uses the metaphor of Breath. Liebenow suggests, "to breathe into the grief you feel in this moment (oxidize it) and exhale. Breathe in fresh energy and breathe out what is burned up. When sharing stories of your loved ones with others, this breathes life back into them. Let them bring you joy again. Even though progress might seem agonizingly slow, each day we are breathing our way through grief." (Liebenow, 2018, para. 11).

Exercise 1: "Where are You Now" Checklist.
Please take some time to go through this list and check all feelings that have come up for you in this past month. It's important to periodically check in with ourselves to see what is coming up for us and where we are in our grief process.

"Where are You Now" Checklist

Below is a list of feelings one might experience while grieving.
Check ALL that have applied in the past month.

☐ Numb	☐ Overwhelmed	☐ Bitter
☐ Sorrow	☐ Obsessed	☐ Confused
☐ Lost	☐ Bottling it up	☐ Relief
☐ At Peace	☐ Guilt	☐ Helpless
☐ Detached	☐ Calm	☐ Self Doubt
☐ Despair	☐ Controlling	☐ Resolve
☐ Euphoria	☐ Shocked	☐ Anxious
☐ Crazy	☐ Shame	☐ Isolated
☐ Lonely	☐ Worried	☐ Angry
☐ Dread	☐ Blame	☐ Sad
☐ Happy	☐ Excited	☐ Longing
☐ Avoidance	☐ Preoccupation	☐ Accident-Prone
☐ Hopeless	☐ Fear	☐ Forgetful

CHAPTER 2

Waves of Grief: How to Be With the Pain and Heal

Feeling leads to momentary pain and permanent relief.
~ Chinese Proverb

Joy and pain are held the same in the body. A person cannot experience one without experiencing the other. Sometimes one is holding both at the same time. This seems impossible, yet it is. In my work as a grief counselor, I can't tell you the number of times that grieving people have told me they were afraid of being with the pain. The clients mention a fear of getting stuck in the pain or not being able to survive the intensity of the pain. Because of their various fears they would find any way to avoid the pain. However, the one thing that holds true, is that no matter how much we want to push the pain away and avoid, it is there waiting. Avoiding the pain can only be done for a period of time before it all bubbles up and we are flooded, not only with the pain of a new loss, but with the pain from any previous, unresolved loss. "Suppression leads to momentary relief and permanent pain. Feeling leads to momentary pain and permanent relief." (Chinese Proverb).

I am going to give you a metaphor that has been used time and time again in the world of grief work. It is helpful in understanding the value of being with the pain and working through it for complete healing.

Surfer. Photo Credit: Paul Dunkley

I'll start with a personal story. When I was maybe 13 years old, I went on a family trip to Maui, which was quite an adventure for this Oklahoma girl! Well, I had a swimming pool at home and swam every day. So, how different could the ocean really be? I was wearing my new prescription sunglasses. I went in for a swim. Suddenly, what felt like a monster wave just took me into it, tumbled me all around and spit me back out. My whole world was rocked, sunglasses gone, sand in every crevasse. I remember walking back to the beach in total shock, dazed from what had just happened.

This was the scariest thing that had ever happened in my 13 years, by far. But, lo and behold, I am here today to tell about it, and since that day, I have experienced a great many more waves, with increasing grace and ease.

Going into the pain of grief is much like going into a wave like that in the ocean for the first time. Not knowing what to expect, it can be shocking. Will I come out alive? Will I survive this? If you have experienced a wave, you know that if you just go with the wave and ride the wave, it will pass over you leaving you safe and feeling that you have gone through something, succeeded. You feel better and you feel different. If you just trust the process of healing, be with the waves of grief, and let them pass, you will truly and fully heal. Nobody wants to be with the pain, but in order to truly heal, we must allow ourselves to feel.

The **Loops of Recovery Graph** was created by Mary Ransom, and is described more in depth in her book "Courage Road." Ransom says, "The following graph is an important piece of information about how the healing process goes.

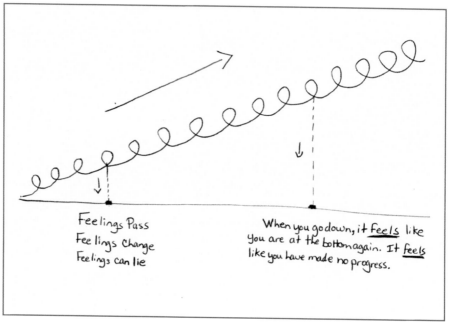

Feelings Pass
Fee lings Change
Feelings can lie

When you go down, it <u>feels</u> like You are at the bottom again. It <u>feels</u> like you have made no progress.

Loops of Recovery Graph

"Remember that healing is not a straight line upward. When you start to go upward, that feels good, but be aware that there will be a downward loop. The down loop makes you feel that you are starting at rock bottom. This is not true because feelings pass and feelings change. Trust the healing process."

Songwriter Tori Amos wrote, "Healing takes courage, and we all have courage, even if we have to dig a little to find it."

CHAPTER 3

Trauma: Approaches to Healing

We cannot heal what we cannot visualize.

~ Robin Cooper-Stone

Psychological trauma may set in after a deeply distressing or disturbing experience. Depending on how distressing, one could experience extreme anxiety or Post Traumatic Stress Disorder (PTSD). Overcoming severe trauma is possible. The use of tools to integrate the left and right brain through the use of the senses is a proven effective means of healing. Though there are many approaches to healing PTSD, I will introduce you to two: Eye Movement Desensitization Reprocessing (EMDR) and art therapy. For the purposes of this self-help book, I am only giving an introduction to EMDR for informational purposes. A therapist trained in EMDR can employ this technique if you want to try it.

With regard to the brain, the amygdala (the primitive non-verbal part of the brain responsible for basic emotions) is where meaning first gets attached to an experience. When trauma or a negative event occurs, the processing of that memory in the brain's hippocampus (reasoning and language area) may be incomplete, and certain negative thoughts, feelings, images, or body sensations of that event can get stuck. The brain's prefrontal cortex (executive functioning and decision-making area) may enable us to understand that an event is from the past. A "trigger" (a sight, sound, touch, taste, or smell) will recreate the event as if it happened yesterday. This recurrence in the mind is often accompanied by initial irrational feelings. A rape survivor, for example, may "know" (hippo-prefrontal cortex) that rapists are responsible for their crimes, but this information doesn't connect with the "feeling" of shame or personal blame for the attack.

Eye Movement Desensitization Reprocessing (EMDR) is a psychotherapy treatment created by Francine Shapiro PhD in the 1980's. It is a technique of bilateral stimulation (the use of visual, auditory, or tactile external stimuli occurring in a rhythmic side to side pattern) that helps alleviate distress by processing bits of distressing memories through a joining process. Learning takes place when new associations (insights) with regard to the memory are connected with pre-existing material already in the brain about this memory. It is at this time that the experience is then stored with appropriate emotions. The end goal with EMDR is that the person no longer feels as if

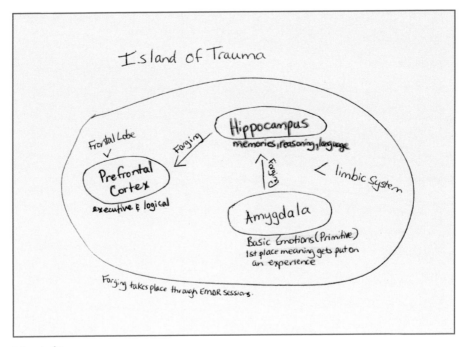

Island of Trauma

they are "reliving" an event that took place, but rather recalling this event as something that happened to them in the past.

Mechanical brain

During EMDR therapy the client attends to emotionally disturbing material in brief sequential doses while simultaneously focusing on an external stimulus. Therapist-directed lateral eye movements, such as having the client follow with their eyes an object (such as a finger or pencil) going back and forth while recalling a certain memory, is commonly used, but there are a variety of other stimuli used, including hand-tapping and audio stimulation (Shapiro, 1991).

See Illustration: "Island of Trauma" graph that visually shows how this works. Each circled part of the brain demonstrates an Island, and the arrows to each demonstrate the process of them joining together with new insight and learning through the process of bilateral stimulation.

Art therapy: We express the soul or our inner self through art. Emotions and feelings that we are not able to verbalize through words can represent themselves through colors, lines, textures, and collaged images. It feels so satisfying to let this inner part of us have its

Left/right side brain

"voice," to let it take its "journey" in its own creative way.

The left hemisphere of the brain is identified with language and speech, while the right hemisphere is identified with feelings and emotions, the nonverbal part.

Integration of the two sides of the brain requires use of all the senses. (McNamee, 2004). "The body keeps the score of the emotional experience." (van der Kolk cited in Malchiodi 2003, p. 20).

Memories are stored in the limbic system, our emotional center in the brain. Once a memory from the brain is externalized through an art process of some sort, or finding a particular magazine image that you are drawn to, then you can begin to talk about it or write about it using your left brain. You begin to put words to this once unconscious, stored information. It takes integration from verbal and nonverbal parts to activate all of our senses and put words to this subconscious raw emotion. When we do begin finding words, they often come in the form of metaphor. (Malchiodi, 2003).

Here is an illustration from a griever whose father died a traumatic death when he was a child. A few years later when he was a teenager, through art therapy, he was able to start to process the trauma and begin to heal. This illustration is a three-part drawing completed over several sessions along with the narrative in the teenager's own words.

The teenage boy was directed to express life before death, after the death, and now. Robin Cooper-Stone (cited in Frost, 2010, p. 150), a SoulCollage® Facilitator

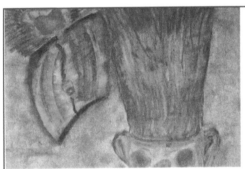

6/23/09 (3 part drawing)
Part 1: Life before death of father. The door to his mind was open allowing for good and bad dreams to occur. Remembers good times with his family (Mexican fiestas, uncles playing cards, music, kids playing tag, soccer with father)
Part 2: After the death. Door to memories was locked and the key was lost. Dreams were always bad, nobody to talk to, nobody understood, poverty set in. Tried to push it all deep inside trying to not remember, think about it.
Part 3: Now. Good, bad, sad, happy is all flowing out of mind. Just at the tip of the surface trying to find the key. At the top of the overflow is the end, when the key will be found. When he reaches this place in the healing process, he will be able to finally talk with his family about the death of his father (Chalk and Pastel)

3 part drawing

who has experienced her own trauma, said, "We cannot heal what we cannot visualize. The very act of finding images brings trauma into the realm of the soul. There the trauma can be confronted, worked with, and accommodated, so eventually it loses its terrifying, Godlike power. This is a part of integration. Trauma becomes merely one of many life events instead of the central event that controls the way we live afterwards."

It is here, in this section about Trauma, that I feel it is important to touch briefly on the topic of suicide and provide a resource. Maybe you have lost a loved one to suicide? A son, daughter, mother, father, sister, brother, friend? Maybe you personally have considered suicide as an option to escape what Kevin Hines, survivor of attempted suicide, coins "lethal emotional pain." Let me just tell you a little about Kevin Hines, whom I recently had the opportunity to see speak live in Santa Barbara, CA. September 2019. In 2000 at the age of 19, two years after being diagnosed with Bipolar Disorder, Hines was dealing with a negative internal dialogue that was telling him that he was not worthy and that he should jump off the Golden Gate bridge. He had people who loved him dearly, cared about him so much, and even the day that he decided to take that leap, Hines recalls his father trying to connect with and support him, yet Hines was doing what he calls, "silencing his pain," keeping this negative internal dialogue that only he could hear, to himself. So, he put those thoughts into action and jumped. Only 1% of people survive that fall and he was one of them. He shared that during that four-second fall, he wished that he had not acted upon those thoughts.

Suicide: Kevin Hines is a great resource for survivors of suicide (those who have lost a loved one to suicide) and those struggling with their own negative internal dialogue. He speaks around the world about suicide awareness and prevention. Hines talks about the "art of living mentally healthy" and that thoughts don't have to lead to actions. He says the use of four simple words, which he still admittedly uses when he needs to be heard, will save your life. Just say, *"I need help now"* and keep saying it until somebody hears you and listens. He says, "We can't bring those back who have died, but we can help those still here to stay alive, and learn the art of living mentally healthy."

Kevin Hines wrote a book titled *Cracked Not Broken: Surviving and Thriving after a Suicide Attempt* (2013) if you are interested in learning more about his story and journey. I also want to include here the National Suicide Hotline: 1-800-273-8255. If you are reading this now, and feeling this way, please use those four words, "I need help now," and don't silence your pain. Find someone to talk to who will listen and support you in this moment right now. You are worthy, you are loved. We are all just human beings trying to navigate through life, through this world and all of the feelings and emotions that come with it. ***Remember that feelings come and go, feelings pass, and feelings change.*** For more information and resources from Kevin Hines, go to: **www.KevinHinesstory/resources.**

CHAPTER 4

Connecting Mind to Body by Awareness of Our Five Senses and Their Power to Heal

"Lose your mind, and come to your senses."
~ Fritz Perls

Revisiting the five senses (vision, hearing, touch, taste, and smell) is a first step to rediscover the "gut feeling" in the grieving process.

The five senses play a critical role in healing and retraining the mind to listen to the inner self. As children, we discovered our environment through our senses and experienced them fully. Every new sensation was amazing. As children we listened to our bodies. Think back to playing in the sand, feeling the grit between your toes, feeling and seeing the texture and color of the grains, seeing the sand stacked and manipulated into mud pies, hearing the sand sift through your hand and fall to the ground, smelling the ocean. As older children, we would see and study an interesting leaf, study the colors in the sky, take time to close our eyes and listen to the sounds of nature. These sensations over time become common everyday experiences and lose their uniqueness and power.

Understanding the physiology and psychology of the senses brings new insight and discoveries. And it's important to keep in mind that there are differences in bodily make ups and past experiences; therefore, different individual reactions can be expected with the senses (color, smell, taste, hearing, etc.) and their overall effects.

Dolphin Photo Credit: Paul Dunkley

Vision: How we see the world visually during grief is just as individual as each person experiencing it. We take in the world through scenes, snapshots consisting of colors, patterns and shapes that not only psychologically tie into memories, but physiologically can create shifts in our body.

Several experiments have shown that different colors affect blood pressure, pulse and respiration rates as well as brain activity and biorhythms. As a result, colors are now used in the treatment of a variety of diseases. (Gruson, 1982, para. 6).

The color blue, for example, is considered a calming and cooling color. Blue rays are said to increase metabolism and promote growth. Blue is balancing and can return the bloodstream to normal when it has become overactive and inflamed, and reduces nervous excitement. It is said to decrease respiration and lower blood pressure. Green, also a cool color, is considered to be soothing and calming, acting as an emotional stabilizer and pituitary stimulant. It is helpful with sleeplessness, exhaustion, and irritability (Hoss, 2005).

Cave Photo Credit: Paul Dunkley

Red and Orange on the contrary are considered warm colors and can excite the body, stimulating the nerves creating an increase in blood pressure. Red rays produce heat that vitalizes and energizes the physical body. Some examples include saunas, dance clubs. Therefore, if one is feeling sad and/or under stimulated, it would be balancing to surround yourself by brighter warmer colors such as red and orange. On the other hand, if you are feeling anxious/over stimulated, then warm colors such as red might act as an irritant to your body, and it would be balancing to surround yourself with blues and greens to provide calm and relaxation (Hoss, 2005).

Hearing: We are constantly inundated by sounds from our environment. Take a moment to just shut your eyes and listen with your ears. Take in every sound you hear. What did you notice? We get so acclimated to the sounds around us that we start to tune out. At times this certainly can be a healthy coping mechanism when it is a sound that associates psychologically with a bad memory, for example. At other times by tuning out, we could miss out on the healing benefits to our body and soul provided naturally in our environment. By gaining a better understanding of the inner work-ings of this sense, comforts and triggers associated with it, we can use the hearing organ to our benefit in healing.

Painting of boy with headphones

With regard to hearing, one perceives different sounds and pitches through a method of energy transfer. Although sound originates from the motion or vibration of an object, it is not the actual vibration of that object that we hear but the effect of that vibration. Our ears alert us to events in the environment. Our ears detect sound waves, which are changes in air pressure; the changes in pressure then travel to our ear and are experienced as sound. (Fincher, 1985).

Let's talk about the power of music! Most can relate to music in some way. The same part of the brain used to process sound is used to process musical

Mayan man playing ukulele

Photo Credit: Harmony Moon Photography

vibration, so even someone who is born deaf can feel and experience different vibrations and rhythms. Why do certain sounds, vibrations, beats, paces of music, voices, make us feel a certain way (happy, sad, angry)? Not only do the words speak to our soul, but the sounds and vibrations do as well.

Barry Goldstein, a composer, producer, and researcher on the vibrational effects of music, wrote a beautiful and informative article on music and its effect on our mood and mind. Research indicates that music stimulates emotions through specific brain circuits. Goldstein talks about how music and the brain engage mood and emotion. "Listening to music can create peak emotions, which increase the amount of dopamine, a specific neurotransmitter that is produced in the brain and helps control the brain's reward and pleasure center. We often feel emotions are experienced from our heart, but an enormous part of emotional stimulus is communicated through the brain. Our newfound understanding of how music affects the brain and heart is leading to innovative ways to utilize music and the brain to create emotional understanding between people. Studies show that music is able to bridge the heart and brain. Music can evoke the deepest emotions in people and help us process fear, grief, sadness,

Man playing drum at subway station

and resentment, even if these emotions are held at a subconscious level." (Goldstein,2018, para. 4).

Based on personal background and our individual life story and journey, music can positively or negatively engage our attention. Goldstein introduces a variety of ways to learn how to use music to positively affect one's mood, help with relaxation, increase focus and attention. These include singing a song, drumming, chanting, playing a song that ties to a positive memory and learning how to play an instrument. Playing an instrument for example engages both left and right brain. One uses the left

Accordion and boy
Photo Credit: Harmony Moon Photography

side for the technical part of learning to play an instrument while the right side is engaged as creative ideas start flowing.

Goldstein talks about how different frequencies induce different states in our brain, therefore depending on what wave frequency one is currently experiencing, their mood will be affected differently by music beats, sounds and vibrations. Goldstein states that it is important to understand the four wave frequencies in order to incorporate music that will ultimately be transformative and healing. *Beta Waves* give an effect of being awake/normal alert, engaging in work is an example. In this frequency, individuals are in fast pace, dealing with work and family. *Alpha Waves* give an effect of being calm, relaxed, meditating or taking a break from work. *Theta Waves* produce deep relaxation and meditation, mental imagery or daydreaming, as examples. *Delta Waves* are an effect of deep, dreamless sleep, and an example is REM sleep.

Closing one's eyes or listening to calm music are examples of ways to move from the fast pace state of beta waves to a more relaxed brain wave state, the alpha state of mind, bringing a calmer mood. Goldstein shares that as one travels to a deeper state of relaxation, helped by meditation and relaxing music, the shift goes into the theta brain wave state. He shares, "It is in alpha and theta states that we tap into enhanced creative frames of mind. As our bodies progress into deep sleep, we are in delta and our brain waves have fully slowed down." Therefore, we can set our intentions. If one wants to move into a creative state, utilizing music with alpha and theta frequencies is suggested. If one wants to get relief from insomnia, incorporating music with delta frequencies will be beneficial. Barry Goldstein, among other composers, has scientifically designed music to incorporate different targeted brain wave states. "Integrating music is a transformative pathway to heal and improve our minds." (Goldstein, 2018, para. 37).

Touch: Through the skin organ, healing of the body is accomplished from the outside in through touch. Especially in a time of grief, when the body has been overworked emotionally and physically, it is important to give yourself some love

Body immersed in water Photo Credit: Paul Dunkley

and attention. Massage, acupuncture, swimming, showers, water therapy, and wrapping up in comfortably textured fabrics are ways you can do this.

Humans need touch and connection. This too is different for each person based on personal experience. Someone who has experienced physical or sexual abuse may fear touching. The goal then would be to explore healthy and safe ways to incorporate touch.

For those who experience high levels of anxiety, a specially designed weighted blanket helps to calm nerves and relax the body. There are a variety on the market, but one in particular known as the Mosaic weighted blanket can be custom-made for children or adults alike. The company describes

Apple

an instant feeling of being hugged when putting the blanket on.

The Skin Organ is the boundary that separates the inside of the body from the world. It is tough, therefore; protects our internal organs from chemical and environmental exposure, yet it is soft and sensitive enough to respond to the gentlest touch. The body of an adult is comprised of around 65% water, a little more at birth.

Though skin is a barrier and barricades some toxic substances, it secretes fluids that lubricate it and absorbs other substances, particularly those soluble in oils. Skin is also a prominent part of the body's temperature-regulating system. It is an ongoing job to maintain a core body temperature of around 98.6 F in order for the internal organs to function properly. (Fincher, 1985). Therefore, it is important to drink plenty of fluids, and stay hydrated at all times. In a time of grief, sometimes the most basic of needs such as drinking enough fluids gets neglected, which leads to other issues such as our inability to stay regulated, to function and think clearly.

Taste: The sense of taste plays a larger role in the grieving process then is often consciously noted. We, as humans often turn to food, not only for physical nourishment, but for emotional comfort. Therefore, taste is both a physiological and psychological experience. For example, certain foods not only taste good on the palette, but depending on the food source may be associated with feelings of love and nurturing, for example grandma's chicken noodle soup.

On the flip side, we can also avoid giving ourselves the food and nourishment our body needs for a variety of reasons such as the psychological state of our mind, or having a bad reaction to a food/drink that created a bad memory associated with it, such as when we feel the after-effects of eating too many sweets, food poisoning, or certain medications. I recall getting so sick at a girl scout's meeting in the 3rd grade after eating burned cookies. To this day, I have an aversion to a cookie that is even slightly crisp.

Also, emotional stress can further take a physical toll on our bodies in that it can lead to health conditions such as stomach ulcers, which in turn make it more challenging to get the nutrition that our body needs to sustain itself. Foods that might have given pleasure before now create such a disposition for us that we avoid what was once comforting.

According to Rochelle Bilow, both mind and body are involved in the way taste is perceived and experienced. "While the response may be the immediate result of a physical factor (the body), salivating, it rounds out as a strong nostalgic reaction (the mind). Sugar from a chocolate chip cookie might give a jolt of joyful energy and rev our salivary glands, but it always tastes better if it comes from a nurturing place like mom's kitchen." (Bilow, 2014, para. 15).

"Tasting experiments have shown that different regions of the tongue have characteristically different levels of sensitivity to the four basic taste sensations: sweet, sour, salt and bitter. The sensory response to different types of molecules, centered on the taste buds of the tongue, is a vital part of total taste perception. A characteristic contour map of the surface of the tongue shows that the sides have peak sensitivity to acidic tastes, the front tip to sugars, while the back of the papillate zone of the tongue is most sensitive to bitterness." (Fincher, 1984, p. 86-87).

Smell: My grandmother died when I was 11 years old. When I was around 30 years old, I was just walking along in a crowd of people, when I took in a smell that instantly rewound my brain to being in the funeral home sitting with my grandmother's body saying my last goodbyes. It took a short bit to register why that memory popped in my brain, but then it came to me. The smell that returned

me to that early memory was of the make-up foundation that had been used on my grandmother; and this was the exact smell I registered almost 20 years later from someone in that crowd wearing the same make-up foundation.

Of all of our senses, smell is the most primal, but is also quite complex. Smell, a chemical sense, communicates not only pleasures in life, but also

Rose Photo by Ergita Sela on Unsplash

signals danger. "An interesting fact: to identify the smell of a rose, the brain analyzes over 300 odor molecules. The average person can discriminate between 4,000 to 10,000 different odor molecules." (Newton, 2000, para. 4). Odor molecules travel through the passage between your nose and mouth to olfactory receptor cells at the top of your nasal cavity. An impulse is generated which is passed to the brain along the olfactory nerve. It arrives first at the olfactory bulb. Once the signal is processed there, the information about the smell travels to the limbic system.

The sense of smell is the sense that has the strongest association to the limbic system, the part of the brain associated with memories. Odors access strong memories of people, places, and events in our lives. This explains why smell plays such an important role in memory, mood, and emotion. (Fifth Sense, 2015).

We all have different tolerances and sensitivities to our sensory organs. Factors include: personal background/experiences, side effects of medication that alter the senses, positioning on the autistic spectrum, and the strength or weakness one has in a particular sense. All of these play a role in how information is received and processed in the limbic system, as mentioned above, in the part of the brain scientists believe plays a major role in controlling mood, memory, behavior, and emotion.

In summary, we are all built differently. One person might be extra sensitive to high pitches, whereas someone else might prefer them. With regard to touch, what feels like hot water to one person, may actually feel just lukewarm or even cold to another. One person might prefer the texture of the rough side of a blanket, while another prefers the soft silky side. While one person finds the experience of being by the ocean comforting, another might find it unpleasant.

When we consider and understand these differences within our close relationships, we will better understand and support each other's individualities in our journeys together. I mention this because in grief, as each family member is affected by the loss of a loved one, we can remember that each also experienced a unique relationship with the lost loved one and will be affected in an individual way. Each had different experiences and will tell different stories about that person. All will grieve differently and all ways are okay.

CHAPTER 5

Grounding and Mindfulness Exercises to Prepare for the Deeper Soul Work

"Mindfulness is a way of befriending ourselves and our experience."

~ Jon Kabat-Zinn

Setting Intentions

Let's start this chapter by setting some intentions. As Sharon Salzberg quotes in her book *Real Happiness: The Power of Meditation,* "Let the breath lead the way" (2011, p. 47). One breath at a time, one second at a time. Be okay with wherever you are in this moment, and let go of any expectations. You woke up this morning; Breathe that in. If all you can do today is just sit in a chair or lie in bed, be okay with that. Listen to what your body is telling you, what it needs at this moment. A warm shower, a snuggly blanket, a hug, a calming image to retrieve, a soothing song or meditation, or maybe it needs a good workout, a brisk walk, a surf, a round of golf, some yoga?

Sometimes our body shuts down as a way to protect us, to avoid a reality we are not yet ready to take in, and this is okay. But life is a balance, so, as with anything, if this avoidance goes on for a period of time, it is important to reach out to a friend, a counselor or a trusted support to help guide you through.

This first series of exploratory exercises is designed to provide a foundation for truly healing from within. The exercises assist with rediscovering your gut feeling, tuning in to and hearing your body tell you what it needs in a new way.

Exercise 2: Daily Journal–Noticing Responses to Environment Exercise.

For one week carry around a notepad or journal, and a writing utensil. Each day notice shifts of mood and make note of the sensory experience related to the mood.

Being mindful and listening to the body and the senses may be difficult. Be patient with yourself. As soon as a mood shifts, ask yourself who or what brought about the unpleasant (trigger) or the pleasant (comfort) response. What memory or trigger was stirred? Was it a smell? Was it a sound like the tone of a voice, music, car horns? Maybe it was something you saw, like the ocean, the hospital, or a person? Or was it a touch, like the way the wind hit your face, the feel of being in water, the way you were or were *not* touched in a loving or non-loving way? Note this in your journal. As you continue to write in your daily journal, you can begin to work on the next exercise.

Exercise 3: Comforts/Triggers Worksheet.

This exercise (see next page) will give you the opportunity to write examples of both comforts and triggers associated with each sense. Again, this process is ongoing and might start off very slow, but it is an important foundation for bringing awareness to and moving through grief. Remember, everybody has different comforts and triggers based on the personal background and experience of each.

These exercises will not only bring awareness of what calms and re-focuses you, but also what to avoid or have less of in your life until you are better equipped to handle it in a healthy way. Often in a state of grief, at any given moment, we can be "triggered" by a sound, smell, or other sensory stimulus and be caught completely off guard. Often this is at an unconscious level, so we may not even be able to associate with words what just shifted our happy mood to angry, anxious mood to calm. Other times we might know exactly what created a mood shift,

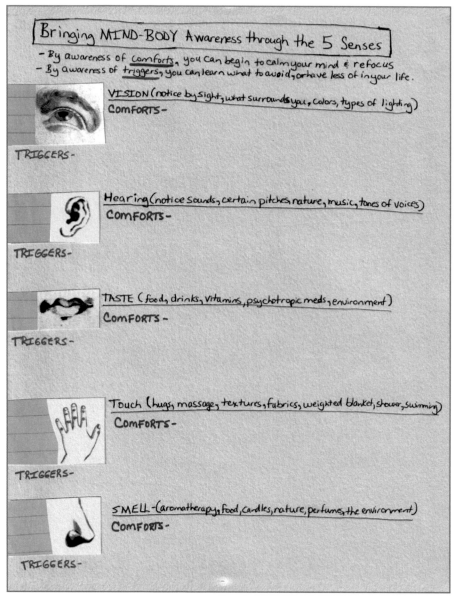

Bringing Mind-Body Awareness through the 5 senses worksheet

such as the smell of aftershave worn by one's late husband or a song on the radio that stirs a memory, cigarette smoke, alcohol, the sight of an ambulance, the smell of the ocean, or a smell that reminds you of your childhood home.

Once completing this exercise, think about how you could change your immediate environment to make it more soothing and comforting to you. Think of the rooms in your home. Which one do you feel most relaxed in, most energized in? Is there a particular space that makes you feel uneasy or unpleasant? Are there changes that you could make to help you feel more relaxed and safer? Sometimes just a minor adjustment can make all the difference in the world such as adding, removing, rearranging or changing colors, wall art, photos, aromatherapy, certain objects, music, or touch, such as textures. For example, having a favorite soothing blanket or sheets for your bed, or wearing clothing that comforts your skin.

Exercise 4: Comfort Journal.

What is a Comfort Journal?

Grounding and calming the body is a basic first step before beginning your healing work. This grounding allows you to "be with the pain" and work through it with safety nets in place.

When we are in a state of distress, it is difficult to be logical and recall what is helpful, what has worked in the past to calm our heart, soul and mind. When the body is over-stimulated; the mind will often race out of control. A comfort journal is a journal that you create full of various materials (photographs of people, places and objects that are grounding, magazine clippings, words, cut outs of textures that

Cover page

In this section are examples of a comfort journal. There is no right or wrong way to do this. It is an individual process.

are comforting, encouraging affirmations and quotes, lyrics or list of comforting or meaningful songs, photograph of an album cover, list of favorite movies) that bring a sense of peace, safety and comfort. The materials in this book are to be reminders to you of how to become

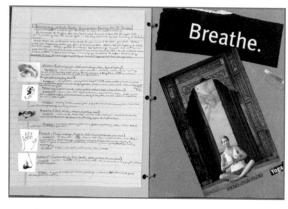

Breathe

grounded again when feeling scattered and overwhelmed. This journal will include representation of comforts for each sense that you have already discovered in the previous exercises as well as new ones you discover along the way. As Cathy Malchiodi states in her book, "The Soul's Pallette: Drawing on Arts Transformative Powers for Health and Well being" in a similar exercise that she presents, titled the "Self Soothing Image Book", "Images are a simple way to move yourself from a stressful state to one of calm or to give yourself a relaxation break." (2002, p.155) The journal can be made with any size paper and with any type of material.

Using Your Comfort Journal

You will then have a visual resource you can go to. You can open your comfort journal to help you come back to the here and now. Once this exercise is completed, this is a journal that you will want easy access to. Make copies in a few different siz and place them where

Vetiver oil

you will have easy access wherever you are in your day. Maybe it would be nice to make a small one that could fit into a purse or pocket. Or maybe a larger one that can be placed on your night stand or coffee table.

When you feel overwhelmed, pick your comfort journal up and use it as a resource. Choose something out of your journal and do it. Play a favorite song, take a

Horses/nature

warm shower, cozy up in a blanket of your choice, use essential oils, call a friend, take a walk in nature, surround yourself with colors that will provide the calm and balance you need in that moment based on what you have learned about your own individual needs.

Opening your comfort journal will immediately help you shift your mood and start to calm your nerves so that your mind can refocus. It's amazing how the mind gets in the way, to talk you out of listening to the body responses. Let your comfort journal make suggestions. Then, when you are ready, just get up and *do* them!

Exercise 5: Mind-Body Scan

Before moving more deeply into healing soul work, it is important to identify supports and challenges in your life. Getting this information out of your head and onto paper is a useful visual tool. This exercise allows you to evaluate all areas of your life. Think about your surrounding environment and what you encounter on a daily/weekly basis. What, who, where do you feel the most safe, nurtured, and loved. In addition, what, who, where are challenges and stresses. Complete the following exercise, being sure to incorporate the five senses into the categories. Please keep in mind that there may be a person, place or thing that falls into both categories (Supports and Challenges) simultaneously. For example, you might have a friend who provides support and nurtures you in some ways, but in other ways might just completely deplete you. So it is good to bring awareness to the ways that your needs are or are not met by the elements in your immediate environment so that you know when and when not to expose yourself to a particular person or situation in your life. Another example might be the overindulgence of a particular food that provides initial comfort, but ultimately causes discomfort in the end like eating a pint of Ben and Jerry's ice cream.

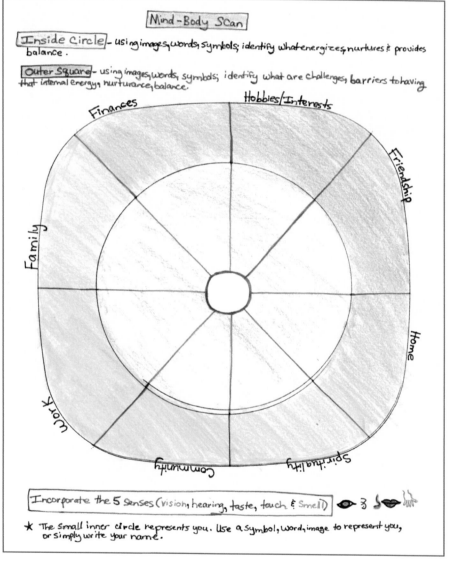

Mind/Body Scan worksheet

Man and woman with Om symbol

Pregnant woman mandala

Exercise 6: Mandala Exercise. What is a Mandala?

In a time of grief, there are moments when one can feel overwhelmed by just the routine of day to day life. The act of creating a mandala from scratch or simply coloring a pre-existing mandala helps provide peace and balance, helps with stress reduction, and can help one become more focused when feeling scattered from struggling with personal issues. Making a mandala simply means creating an image within any circular space.

Mandala in Sanskrit means Magic Circle. Mandalas are a creative form of meditation that have been used since the earliest human history in many cultural and religious traditions as a spiritual practice. Self-created mandalas are reflections of your inner self in the moment and are symbolic of your potential for change and transformation. There are an array of mandala books and resources on the market and some are included in the resource section of this book.

For this exercise, the reader could either choose a pre designed mandala to color or create your own from scratch. This should be relaxing. Do not put pressure on yourself about how the mandala should look, but rather, just let it take you where it takes you.

When creating from scratch, first, identify the center of the circle. Fill in the circle in any way you want, using colors, lines, shapes and designs. Start in the center and work out or start at the edges of the circle ending up in the middle.

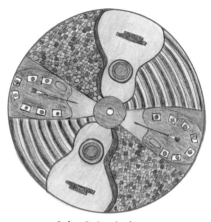

Color Guitar/palette

Guitar/palette in pen

Most importantly, there is no right or wrong way to draw/create your mandala, so add to your drawing until you feel it is complete. No need to censor yourself as this is unique to you. If you are having trouble getting started, draw some type of symbol, such as a heart for example in the middle and work from there.

A Mandala Guided Imagery (Circles of Support). The following exercise (see below) I adapted from Kate Webb, an art therapist in the San Diego, California area. This guided imagery starts with a breathing exercise to help get into the space of the here and now. This is followed by a short meditation before beginning the exercise. I would suggest recording this and then playing it back for yourself, with soft meditative music in the background, so that you can truly have the experience.

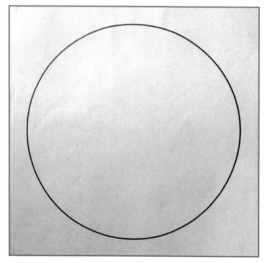

Mandala empty circle

GUIDED IMAGERY
Circles of Support: Creating Mandalas

Before beginning, sit in a comfortable chair, with your legs uncrossed. If you are sitting at a table, you may rest your arms on the tabletop or let them drop to your lap. Close your eyes and focus on your breath, slowly inhaling and exhaling (pause)

Continue to inhale and exhale slowly and relax the muscles in the area around your jaw. Let your jaw open slightly so that any tension there can flow away from your face.

Relax the muscles in your scalp and neck, letting your head move forward slightly. Relax the muscles in your shoulders and, from there: let the relaxation move down into the muscles of your arms and hands. Continue to feel the tension slip away from your back, over your chest, down to your stomach, and all the way down to the base of your spine.

Let the feeling of relaxation spread to your thighs, knees, and lower legs, down to your ankles and feet until it reaches the tips of your toes.

Start from the top of your head and work down. Take a few moments to scan your body for any part that is not fully relaxed. If you feel any part of your body that is not fully relaxed, take a deep breath and send the breath into that area, imagining warmth and relaxation reaching it. When you exhale, imagine the tension leaving your body with the breath. As you continue to breathe in and out, imagine the breath moving in a circular motion in and out of your body.

(This breathing exercise is from Cathy Malchiodi's book, *The Art Therapy Sourcebook*, p. 74).

The circle is a natural form as it has been an important visual throughout human history extending to the origin of the universe. The spirals and orbits. Galaxies and planets. The cells of the human body have the constant presence of circles.

Imagine the circles and cycles of your life. You at the center of a circle. What transitions, losses, milestones are you currently carrying at your core? What strengths are needed to help you stay centered and balanced?

Begin to let images come to represent your center, your support. Maybe some words come to support you. Allow them to surround you with strength needed to move through this transition. Your circle may include people, animals, the natural world around you, shapes, colors, or words. Allow yourself a few moments in the silence to breathe in this safe circle of support. Be with this support. [Allow a minute or so of silence]

Gradually allow yourself to come back to the room. Let your thoughts, images and experiences return with you if you want them to. When you feel ready, you may open your eyes. You may wish to wriggle your fingers and toes. Allow yourself to stand and stretch as need be.

Now, working in silence (with soft meditative music), immediately begin the process of creating your mandala.

Exercise 7: A Mandala Exercise Designed to Help Process Trauma is Below.

> **Materials needed for this exercise:**
> - Worksheet (below)
> - Magazine images/words
> - Scissors
> - Something to draw with
> - Glue

In this particular mandala exercise, the inner circle represents you and your comfort zone (what calms you, what gives you peace). Let the outer square represent your surrounding environment and the trauma, challenges and triggers you face. Using magazine images, words, designs, shapes, drawing, and writing, fill in the inner circle with comforts and the outer square with challenges, trauma and triggers.

I would encourage you to do some journaling about what comes up for you after this exercise. And please tune in to your needs. If you have a trusted person in your life, a friend or a therapist that you can contact for further support if you get flooded, please have their number handy to call and reach out. Those who care about you truly want to support you, help to comfort you. Trust that and don't go through this alone.

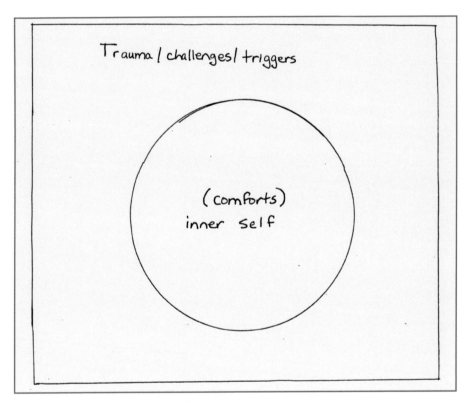

Trauma/Inner support mandala worksheet

Into the Heart of Feelings: Processing Memories through Writing, Drawing and Music

It's not about making art; it's about making a journey.

Let's start with an exercise that involves bringing awareness to your personal strengths and your journey from birth to the present. You may find it helpful to identify on paper, to visually see the list of what specific losses you have journeyed through from birth to present and what strengths you have gathered by doing so before you begin these art and writing exercises.

Strengths & Losses History (Worksheet Follows)

Materials needed for this exercise:
- **Paper or the following worksheet**
- **Something to write with** (Pencil is suggested, but optional)

This exercise requires some unwinding time to retrieve your first childhood memories.

On the left side of the paper (Strengths), list strength memories starting with your youngest age and continuing to current date/age. First memories related to strengths might be of an event or words spoken to you that gave you a feeling of pride, like when a family member tells you that you really did a good job in a particular area of your life, such as a performance or school project. Strengths might also include special moments with family or friends or accomplishments in your life for which you were given an award or singled out. This could be a graduation, marriage, birth(s) of your children, or accomplishments in sports. The mentors in your life or a relative or friend might have pointed out one of your special traits. What significant encouragement and praise can you remember? What pivotal moments that have helped shape you?

On the right side of the paper (Losses), starting with your youngest age of a memory, jot down notes of memories relating to loss and continue to this present time. This does not just mean identifying loss through death such as that of a loved one or special pet, but other losses such as moving to a new town, loss of a friendship, loss of innocence, loss of security, loss of sense of power, loss of feeling capable. This exercise may seem overwhelming and you may experience some resistance, but it is an important exercise to help you move through your grief and identify areas that need further work. Take your time and write as you recall. I also encourage journaling about this exercise after it is completed.

Often times there will be a juxtaposition of losses and strengths coinciding at the same time/age. An example might be that a new baby was born in the same month/year as a loved one died. Therefore on your strengths side of the worksheet would be the birth of a child, while on the losses side would be the loss of a loved one around that same time. Or at one point in life, an event could have been considered a strength and helped shape you, but at a later time in life could become a loss (Marriage/Divorce).

Either use a blank piece of paper or utilize the pre-created form for this exercise starting with age 0 to current age. You may need more than one page to complete this exercise depending on how much life you have lived!

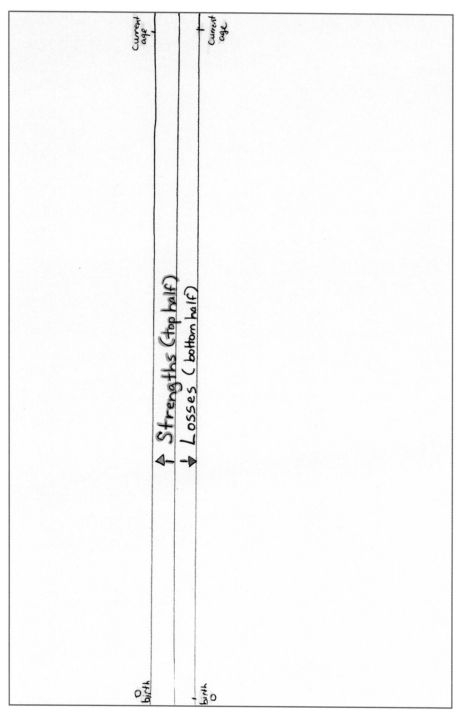

Strengths/Loss Graph

If you do start to feel overwhelmed, I would encourage you to look back at the strengths that you have discovered within yourself and focus on those for a minute. And please take a break and do some self-care, something that helps you feel grounded and aware of the present moment, then come back to this exercise at a later time.

Arts/Crafts Exercises

> **Materials needed for this exercise:**
> - **Paper and something to draw with:**
> - **Crayons**
> - **Markers**
> - **Craypas**
> - **or Colored pencils**

Exercise 8: Scribble Drawing Exercise.

This was developed by art educator Florence Cane. It has been a constant and unwavering art therapy exercise. In art therapy, a great way to incorporate both sides of the brain, all senses, is through the scribble drawing exercise. After completed, the scribble drawing is then given a title as a way for other parts of the brain, the nonverbal parts to tell their story through metaphor. With our left brain, when we are talking or typing, we can edit our story, so it isn't always our full truth, whereas the right brain shares raw emotions on our paper. When we create with the right brain we get a more authentic expression of experience

Breathing Fire

or emotion. What often comes out on paper are images/memories from the brain. (McNamee, 2004). The art that comes when we are using the right brain is all about the evolving process, not the final product (the opposite of the focus of professional art). In these expressive art exercises, there is a shift that takes place between the verbal and nonverbal brain. When you try it, you will begin to understand.

House of Peace

Here's an example: To someone else, the scribble you drew might just be some squiggly lines, something unidentifiable, but to you it might be an image of your childhood dog that died. It takes a little time to make that shift from getting out of our head and into our body and finding the meaning in the art that has come through our right brain.

For this exercise, sit down with your paper and the utensil of choice that you are using to draw with, picking one color, than begin to draw a random scribble without putting thought into it. Then, when you feel that you have enough of a scribble, stop. Now, look at your scribble. See if you can notice anything that looks familiar to you. If not one way, turn your paper, turn again if need be until you find a starting point. Once you have seen something, begin creating. You may add lines, use as many colors as you choose. Just have fun! Once you feel that your scribble is complete, give it a title!

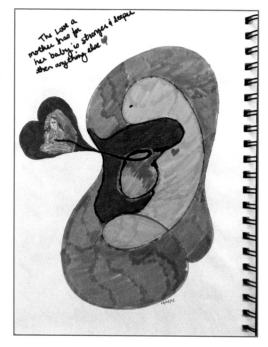

Mother

Tissue paper collage

Exercise 9: Magazine Collage.

Materials needed for this exercise:
- **Paper**   • **Magazines**   • **Glue**   • **Scissors**

Intuitively, cut out images and words from magazines. Arrange them onto a piece of paper of whatever size you choose. I suggest just picking out images that you are drawn to, even if you don't know why, and even if it feels scary or disturbing in some way. The image may be "choosing you" through your right brain. At an unconscious or semi-conscious level, there is a reason for this choice and this will unfold in time. Just trust the process.

Then, after you have completed the collage, step back, reflect, and journal about what you just created. I guarantee after you have done this project, you will start looking at magazine images in a whole new way. I actually got so attached to an image in a magazine one time at the dentist office, I asked if I could rip it out. The receptionist gave me a strange look, but said, "Sure." Hope Floats.

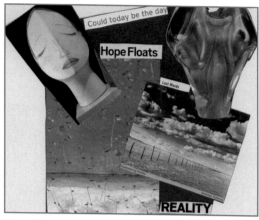

Hope Floats

The language of metaphor created when images from the brain are externalized through art process puts a voice to this once unconscious stored information. (Malchiodi, 2003). Once a memory from the brain is externalized through either art process of some sort or finding a particular magazine image that you are drawn to for example, then you can begin to talk about this or write about it using your left brain, putting words to it. It takes integration from both verbal and nonverbal parts to activate all of our senses and put words to this semi-conscious raw emotion that is accessed through the limbic system, our emotional center that is involved in the formation of memories.

Breathe

Being in the heart of grief is hard work. Please remember to take breaks, to breathe, to take a walk and get some fresh air. When we are in the heart of the pain, we can sometimes feel worse before we feel better, but just know that you will start to feel better. Being able to be with and hold the pain is how the deeper healing begins to take place. Trust the process, and please take care of yourself! Remember to utilize your Comfort Journal when you need it. Fritz Perls wrote, "Pain is meant to wake us up...You feel your strength in the experience of the pain. It all depends on how you carry it."

Exercise 10: Visual Journaling.

Materials needed for this exercise:
- A journal or several pieces of paper
- A whole punch and string
- Images (photographs and magazine images)
- Various writing utensils, glue, scissors

First, What is a visual (art) journal? It is a book created by the artist, a personal expression containing mixed media work, such as collage and painting. It includes writing. It goes as deep as you need it to. You can include photos, stamping, memorabilia, and writing from within. Combining words with imagery is very powerful.

It's not about making art; it's about making a journey. To start, leave internal and external censors outside the door. Let go of expectations, judgment, what you should or shouldn't create, and just let the process unfold. Visual journaling stills the mind and silences the mind's censors and commentators. The hands-on approach allows one to express freely.

Why do it? It is a way to express oneself and work through the full array of feelings (from anger or sadness to joy). It is how we can externalize what is manifesting inside. It's cathartic, a release, a way to actively work through feelings. If one is in a funk, the visual journal is a quick way to shift one's mood, help one get unstuck in order to get energized and centered. After, you will feel calmer and more focused. Working through something intense or painful can be draining, but it is necessary to help move you through the issue. This is for you. Nobody has to see it, so creating all types of pages is an important part of healing.

The journal can be about life experiences (good or bad), along with dreams, goals, and hopes. You can journal about everything, as everything is what makes you who you are today and helps you become who you want to be. It is nice to reflect back on your journal through life to see all that you have overcome and journeyed through. You will be able to look through it later and see how your process of transformation has evolved.

There are a variety of books I have referred to through my own process. They are listed in the index. This book is merely a guide to help you get started. For further exploration and tools in visual journaling, please refer to books from index.

Exercise 11: Altered Book project

> **Materials needed for this exercise:**
> - An existing book that you
>   are okay with altering
> - Photographs, magazine images
> - Glue, scissors, something to draw with

Altering a book is not a new concept, and has been a form of art therapy for some time, though I would like to introduce ways to utilize this project in working through grief. We think of a book as complete, we accept it as finished. This is much how we view life at times, complete, with a clear future already planned out. Then tragedy shakes that foundation leaving us changed, transformed and at a loss for words sometimes. Our hopes, dreams, and expectations all may change.

Road not Taken

New life experiences that provide us with new information can rock our foundations, re-defining our perception of what gives our life meaning. Likewise many books are edited, transformed, and changed in new editions as different generations are exposed to it, or as the author has more life experiences to add.

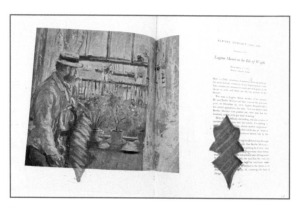

Man looking out window

The altering of a book can be challenging as one may become attached to certain meaning it has, how it is made, and the content. It may be hard to alter that which is already made. But, in altering a book,

Red shape in ocean

we become more comfortable with change. In letting go of one thing, something new may emerge, surprises may happen. The newly altered book is the same in information and content, but is altered, layered, transformed. There may be parts of the book that one never agreed with. We may have had a hard time reading or looking at a particular page or chapter for whatever reason, so that part may need to be removed, separated, and then possibly reincorporated in a new way. We reshape the book.

This is very much like ourselves dealing with grief. It is hard to accept the changes that are happening, feeling like one has little or no control over it, it just is. What gives life meaning is our redefining it.

Just as parts of the book remain, so do parts of our loved ones we have lost.

Clock and Head

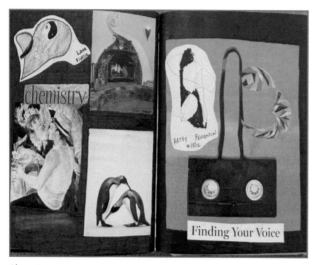

Chemistry

They are a part of us, but just in a different way now. This is an opportunity for all to take a look at the whole person, not just remembering the last year, months or days of the loved one's life, but remembering the whole person. There is still a relationship; it is just that the nature of that relationship has changed. It is much like a book in that one can cover up words on a page, hide them, but they are under the surface. What gave meaning to your life in the past? What gives meaning to your life now? What are your hopes for the future?

Prayer

Exercise 12: Art therapy with a Specific Feeling or Experience in Mind.

Materials needed for this exercise:
- **Choose paper and something to write or draw with**

This is where the person draws or paints using the medium of their choice about a particular topic or feeling, and transfers the images from the mind onto the paper. For example, "what does anger look like."

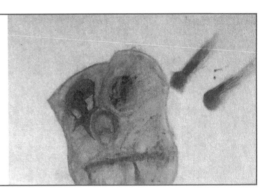

6/02/09 "Initial reaction to loss of father was confused, shocked. Metaphor is about the scar it has created. There is a part of him the world sees (the bright colors) happy, getting on with life, and the other part (vivid red) that is stuck, scarred. Metaphor of scars and how they are always there, but can heal, get smaller, less visible where others don't see the scar, but it is still there." (Pastel)

Initial reaction to loss

The illustration above demonstrates this technique. This Illustration is "recalling the initial reaction when finding out about the loss of his father, in the bereaved teenagers own words."

Graffiti: This is a controversial topic for sure. But one conclusion I have come to from years of working with at-risk teens who are grieving is that graffiti is a creative outlet in which they can express themselves and feel a part of a community by sharing their art; therefore, not feeling alone in their grief. Often those

RIP Photo credit: Paul Dunkley

Guys doing graffiti mural on wall Photo Credit: Flowing River

who start engaging in graffiti come from challenging homes and communities where they have not had healthy coping modeled to them. They crave a sense of belonging in some way.

I am not condoning graffiti that is damaging city buildings and the community. But, there are wonderful community programs (and could be more) that involve teens who enjoy doing graffiti. These programs give permission to these teens

A guy doing skull graffiti mural Photo Credit: Nathalie Gensac

to express their feelings in a healthy way that keeps them out of trouble with the law. In these community programs, teens may work on a group mural with a professional artist helping guide them. Or, they may work on other types of creative expressions of art in community projects that are monitored and designed to enhance the community rather than damage it. This type of program helps provide a safe and connecting environment for individuals and allows them the opportunity to be with others who are going through similar struggles. It is great for building self-esteem as well.

Writing Exercises

> **Materials needed for these exercises:**
> • Paper and a writing utensil

Often there is the notion that if we write something sad, we won't stop crying. A good cry can sure be cathartic and quite healing. Did you know that actually when we release tears, we are releasing toxins from our body. So it is also quite good for our physical health.

Exercise 13: Goodbye or Forgiveness Letter (a Two-part Exercise)

PART 1: It is really not all that common that a person is able to tell their dying loved one what they would have wanted them to know or to resolve unfinished business. Even in those times where we are by the bedside, sometimes for a variety of reasons, we just can't get the words out that we want to convey. Other times, the loss is sudden and unexpected; thereby making an opportunity for closure impossible. The idea behind the goodbye letter is to allow the bereaved individual or the individual in anticipatory grief not knowing how to say good bye to their loved one at the bedside to do it. This gives them the opportunity to formulate some words in a private meaningful way. These words may be shared with the loved one, or not, but they may ultimately help provide some closure. This exercise has been used in Hospice work and, in my opinion, it is a very powerful process.

All you need is paper, a writing utensil and a little bit of time. Phrases that might prompt expression of feelings might include: "I'm angry that...", This is what you meant to me...", I wish I could have told you...", Where are you now?" The letter is written as if you are really having a conversation with this person.

After you finish the letter, you might choose a completion ritual. There are a variety of rituals to embark upon. You could dig a hole in the sand at the beach for example and burn the letter. Some believe that somehow the words will reach wherever the soul has gone. Or, you could keep the letter in a special place.

PART 2: Writing a response letter from your loved one.

When you have written the above letter, you might wonder what your loved one would reply. What would they say back to you? You could write back to yourself, as them, in the voice of your loved one.

Exercise 14: Poetry.

Perie Longo is an LMFT and registered poetry therapist who has, to date, published four books of poetry and poems in numerous literary journals. She has been facilitating poetry writing groups for Hospice of Santa Barbara for many years. Perie says poetry accesses buried emotion quickly, because it is compact, musical, and uses images that speak to the subconscious. It also is a container to hold feelings. In Perie's group, poems by published writers are offered for group participants, to read aloud. The group then discusses lines, phrases, and images that have evoked emotion and memory.

Perie says for example, in the poem "Curtains" by Ruth Stone there is the line, "See what you miss by being dead?" In context, this is humorous and poignant at once, a prompt to write about what the beloved is missing instead of the other way around, what we are missing of them. This emphasizes the importance of the continuance of life. Additional prompts arise from a certain line or phrase spoken during the group discussion, which can start a flow of words. Perie states that in offering feedback to each other, they honor the value of what has been written from their depths. Sharing deeply ensures they are understood—and the group's understanding means that they are not so alone in their grief.

In teen grief groups I have facilitated, a popular type of group poem is started with a title such as "Grief is…," Special Memories with my loved one are…,"

"Anger is…. The participants pass around the paper, each writing one line and folding it over so the previous person does not know what they have written. After going around the group twice or so depending on the size of the group, a participant is chosen to read the whole collected poem. So, there is a bit of mystery as to who wrote what part, but they together have created something amazing. The exercise of picking a title and writing a poem is something that can also be done individually.

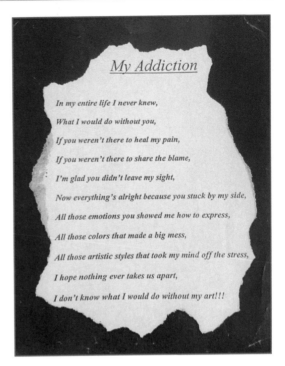

My Addiction

In my entire life I never knew,

What I would do without you,

If you weren't there to heal my pain,

If you weren't there to share the blame,

I'm glad you didn't leave my sight,

Now everything's alright because you stuck by my side,

All those emotions you showed me how to express,

All those colors that made a big mess,

All those artistic styles that took my mind off the stress,

I hope nothing ever takes us apart,

I don't know what I would do without my art!!!

My Addiction poem "My Addiction" was a poem written by a griever who was a teenager at the time. He really found healing through art and writing.

Exercise 15: Free writing.

Materials needed for this exercise:
- Paper, something to write with, and a timer

This is an exercise I have used quite often not only with teenagers, especially those I worked with at Los Prietos Boys camp (a boot camp for troubled teens) but also with adults of all ages. It was quite an effective exercise in helping them tap into unconscious, unresolved feelings, process and let go of thoughts that were weighing them down. It was safe in that it was nonverbal and the paper could be ripped up right afterwards, if they wanted.

Set the timer for 10 minutes. Start writing on the paper. The rules are

The hand-written journal entries read:

Journal entry
11-05-01

A day, a night, a wave
a wave, a rock, a splash
a splash, a seductive breeze,
an orgasmic chill
The warmth of the sun,
the way it makes me feel
Oh so whole
A thought of the warm
desert and the way
a heated rock jolts a
bit of the sun to my
heart
A wave, a chill,
a rock
a cloud
I am an eagle
I am a wave
I am in the earth
and of the stars
But I am merely only
a grain of sand.
Shawn

Journal entry
09-25-06

I see your face in a homeless man.
I call for you but you do not come.
Have you found peace.
Are you part of the cactus that blocks the sun
If I peel off the thorns,
will your soul be released.

I am the earth you grow in.
I am the gentle raindrops
that hydrate you.
I am the clear sunny sky
that looks after you.
I am you.
Release me.
Valerie

Journal entry
10-16-07

LOVE YOU
AND
MISS
you.
Valerie

Sibling Poem

not to stop writing, not to censor or edit, and not to read over what you wrote until the timer bings.

What do I mean by "censor?" Well, we humans constantly edit our responses internally thus censoring our interactions with others. We even censor ourselves personally for a variety of reasons. Censorship ultimately means we aren't being completely honest and true with our feelings.

Your writing in this exercise does not need to make sense in any way or be grammatically correct. If you can't think of anything to write, write just that "I can't think of anything to write..." until the thoughts start to come. After the time is up, read what you have written to yourself, or aloud if you choose. Sometimes it may be better not to read it at all. If that is the case, just destroy the paper in some way, letting this be a process of cleansing and letting go.

It's amazing how often in daily life we censor ourselves with others and even inside ourselves. When writing in other ways, we can still erase, rewrite to convey what we want to, but with free writing, that is not an option. We want free writing to really reflect our honest and true self in the moment.

CHAPTER 7

When Grief Resurfaces

When can grief resurface in a more intense way? It can happen as one approaches holidays, special events, or special dates like birthdays. Environmental changes, weather or a change of seasons can also trigger new grief reactions. Certain experiences can be triggers. The sudden resurgence of thoughts and feelings about your loss can be unexpected, especially if you've recently experienced relief from those more intense feelings and thought you were done.

Some other examples of what might trigger feelings of grief also include dating or wedding anniversaries, day of week or month that diagnosis or death occurred, annual events such as parades, concerts, community gatherings, smells, music or sounds or just the way the wind hits your face!

By predicting what may trigger your grief and planning ahead, you may be able to cope better. Increasing supports can be essential in coping with returning grief. Consider planning ahead for a visit or phone call with family or friends or a support group. Utilize the above exercises in preparing for these either expected or unexpected intense waves of grief that might come. The Mind-Body Scan, the Comfort Journal, and The Awareness of Senses Exercises are all helpful to refer to at times such as these.

There are a variety of ways to create something in your loved one's memory or create some type of ritual that you can do each year following a certain date. After someone dies, there is a focus on the death or the dying process, but a goal might be for you to be able to create about and remember the whole life of the person, not just the last year, days of their life, but the life of the relationship. There is still a relationship; it's just the nature of the relationship that has changed. Refer back to the above exercises and pick one of them to do. Following are some additional exercises to consider trying out:

Exercise 16: Memory Box.
Decorate a box (of any size) using whatever you choose (photo or magazine collage, paint, embellishments, tissue paper, words, etc.) that represents your loved one in some way, reminds you of them, or helps you feel closer to them. This will then be a place to store special memorabilia such as letters, photos, even small gifts they have given you.

Exercise 17: Gift Box.
For this project, one needs a box of any size. This is decorated in whatever way you choose. Then, this box is set up somewhere in your house that everybody has access to in some way. Beside the box would lie pieces of paper and a writing utensil. Anyone who knew the loved one, as they stop by for a visit, could write stories, memories about this person and place them in the box. Then the individual or family doing this project could then pick a special time, such as a birthday, holiday, or a special event, to open the box and read what is inside, sharing stories, laughs, and tears together.

CHAPTER 8

Using SoulCollage® in Grief

What is SoulCollage®?

SoulCollage® is: "a method of self-discovery through creation and intuitive work with a deck of collaged cards." This section offers a brief introduction to this rich and meaningful process of healing. I would encourage those who are interested in pursuing this further, to locate a SoulCollage® Facilitator/workshop in your area or online and experience it firsthand. There are workshops and trainings all over the world for this self-discovery process.

What SoulCollage® is not.... It is important to know that SoulCollage® is not a religion and is neither attached to nor opposed to any

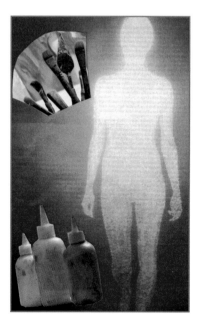

Creativity Card

spiritual system. It is a creative and transformational self-discovery process using images that are placed on matte board (as you can see in the illustrations in this chapter.) It is a method for working with one's own experience of self and spirit.

Swan Card

We are the One and the Many. Our whole being and the many parts of us. We are the mother, the father, the daughter, the son, the grief coun-selor, the grieving self, the funny one, the shy one, the controlling self, the curious child, the wounded child, the anxious self, the creative self. Depending on where we are in our journey, who we are around, what we are doing (work, home, vacation) these different parts come out. Some parts may be hidden, for example parts of self from childhood or other parts of our past, but they are still a part of us. When we look at images, we start reconnecting to those parts.

In SoulCollage® we make a deck of cards having four suits (Committee suit, Community suit, Council suit, and Companions suit). Each card represents a part of ourselves. These cards are made intuitively and express an array of different feelings, including fears, anger, sadness, joy, love, happiness, transition, pain, suffering.

Don't pick the images, but instead, through the projective process, let them pick you. SoulCollage® helps make meaning of our journeys in life. We create a deeper connection with our self for transformation and healing.

I will just provide a brief introduction to the four suits. The *Committee Suit* is the psychological suit, the many parts of us, the inner voices in our head such as Mother, Father, Hurt Child, Jealous One, Rebel, Artist, Teacher, Critic, Controller, Dancer.

The *Community Suit* supports our local story. It contains cards made for the real people and pets in our lives (living or dead). This could be through personal relations such as Mother, Father, School Teacher, Mentor, Counselor. Or it could be someone famous that we feel connected to in some way or inspired by such as a well-known leader, writer, or role model.

The *Council Suit* has cards made for archetypes taking part in our life story, Archetypes are the great patterns or themes of our lives like the Wounded Healer, Earth Woman, Holy Spirit, Warrior, Creativity, Grief, Transformation, or Great Mother/Great Father.

Protector Card

The *Companions Suit* is the energetic suit. It contains cards for the bodily energies that are present for us in the seven energy centers in certain areas of the body. The specific energy is displayed onto the card in the form of an animal (animal helpers).

Seena Frost (1932-2016) was the Founder of SoulCollage.® I was honored to be trained as a SoulCollage® Facilitator by Seena in 2014. Seena was a psychotherapist who began creating this specific self-discovery process in the 1980's. This process emerged in its present form over time from her work with women's therapy groups. Seena's study of the works of Carl Jung, James Hillman and others formed the psychological and spiritual underpinning of this tool.

There are certain guiding principles that are clarified in Seena Frost's book *SoulCollage® Evolving: An Intuitive Collage Process for Self-Discovery and Community.* Only one main voice is represented per card, therefore the collage is usually simple, often only with one main image put onto a new background and glued onto a card. It is recommended not to use words, only images, because words limit the intuitive wisdom that you will draw from the cards each time you use the card. The card-making process can be either intuitive or intentional depending on the suit that is being created. When working with the Community and Companions suit, it is often intentional to some degree. Both left and right brain are involved in this self-discovery process. You will recognize the meaning of some images from the start. More often though you will not consciously know what the meaning is right away, and that's okay too. Hang out in the "don't-know-mind" and watch for what wants to manifest. Let it bubble up… Most importantly, trust the process and have fun!

Peace Card

The Light

How does SoulCollage® help us with grieving?

Significant loss shatters the way we see the world. We have to integrate a new way of being, seek a new identity as we strive to find our non-physical connection with one (s) we've lost.

SoulCollage® can be used to help us illuminate our inner soul in the work of deeper healing. The "shadow" (as C.G. Jung used the term) in a card refers to the part of our form or being that is out of balance, meaning that there is *too much* of a particular energy or quality or *too little*. "Shadow" used this way is not "bad".

All SoulCollage® cards in the four suits have the potential to be shadowed. None of our parts are either good or bad, but they can be out of balance, and when we become aware of this, we can balance them. C.G. Jung also realized that this out-of-balance energy can also hold vital and passionate energy. Only by making friends with the shadowed parts can you reclaim them and move toward wholeness. Pushing away this energy can bring about mental and physical illness. Embrace it and release it, rather than pushing it away. The idea is to work through and with what is torturing us.

Here is the SoulCollage® prompt and some questions to ask your card to let it introduce itself to you, once you have made it:

Example 1: Shattered from Grief Card: (Read October 2013)

I Am One Who...

When did you first come into being?
What is your gift for me?

Then you can journal further.

I will provide two personal examples to demonstrate this process.

"I Am One Who.." mourns the loss of my baby boy, One Who feels incomplete, One Who has a broken heart. *I Am One Who* longs for motherhood, who feels emptiness, who should have a five-month old baby right now.

When did you first come into being? Several years ago in my latter 20's, I was feeling incomplete in my marriage and felt having a child was the answer. I tried to get pregnant, but it did not happen. I got divorced at age 30 and felt complete again, not longing for or wanting a child until I fell in love a few years later. My longing came back, not because "it's what you do when you are married," but because I wanted to share in this beautiful experience with the love of my life. We tried for about 8 months and I grieved not being able to conceive at all. I got pregnant in the Fall of 2012, then lost the baby in utero at 18 weeks, due to unhealthy fetus.

Grief's gift to me: I do not take things for granted and appreciate life even more, for growth, deeper love and friendship. I am better able to support others in their grief journey as I know at a deeper level that deep pain and sorrow of grief and what it feels like as healing takes place, the layers, what happens when it resurfaces and how to get through those moments.

Example 2: Card Titled Control Card: (Read, October 2013)

I Am One Who tries to control situations, one who needs things to happen on time, one who is running out of time to be a mother, one who can't open the door, move the door as it is so heavy, one who is fighting with time, one who wants to feel loved at ease, one who wants more romance, one who wants more security, one who wants to feel special and unique, one who wants to feel deserving, *I Am One Who* is controlling, one who is thinking about tomorrow, one who needs to be heard, one who needs to be in nature more, to breathe more, to just be more, one who needs to let go, one who has anxiety.

When did you come into being? Childhood, at home trying to be the peacemaker when my parents argued, when my brother was getting into trouble. I need to be in control because sometimes on the inside is complete chaos, helplessness, emptiness, loneliness.

What is your gift to me? Control, showing me that I love deeply, I want Peace, I want things to go good (what is good?). I am showing you how much you care about yourself and those who are around you.

It's all about the learning process. There is beauty amidst the control. It is a gift to let go, be in the moment.

It is important to remember that what is so present and true at one point in our life, represented through the cards (parts of ourselves), if read at a later point, may have different answers and may have a different meaning. This is because we are constantly in motion, healing, working through, evolving, changing and transforming as we walk through life. These created cards all represent parts of ourselves, the ones who have led us to who we are and what has made us the person we are today.

As we bring awareness and attention to those tender places in our soul and those parts of self are acknowledged and given attention, we can continue to move forward and grow from what we learn in this truly rich self discovery process of SoulCollage.®

A very common exercise used in SoulCollage® workshops to demonstrate how this first question (*I Am One Who…*) works is this: There is usually an array of images of all sorts laying on a table. The person picks a few images intuitively (not putting too much thought into it) that they are drawn to in some way. These images represent parts of ourselves. We find the meaning for us in speaking *from* an image rather than *about* it.

Anne Marie Bennett, a cancer survivor, really found healing in this process. She shared that what makes SoulCollage® different from other forms of processing is the journaling that one does after making a card. In the SoulCollage® process, she talks about the importance of allowing ALL of your feelings; giving them image and room to breathe. She encourages giving yourself the gift of the journey. So, be open to discover what the gift or lesson each card holds. Let go and let the journey of self-exploration begin.

CHAPTER 9

Self-Care

Those who personally know me would most likely tell you that self-care is what I encourage the most in all of my relationships, both personal and professional. If we don't take care of ourselves and our needs, who will? And without self-care, the challenges we already face in this world can be just that much more over-whelming. In this chapter, I will introduce some ways to tune into your body and care for yourself at a deeper level.

We are born into this world instantly forming connections. Along the way, we meet and interact with people and visit places creating lasting impressions. This could be people with whom we share a short visit, as with a traveler we meet on a train ride exchanging stories and life lessons. It could be those more familiar to us, such as our teachers, mentors, family members and friends, who mold and shape us. Through this journey of life people will come and go, but the one force always near is yourself. It is a 24/7, from birth to death relationship. It is important to learn how to love ourselves, get to know ourselves and enjoy being with ourselves.

If we are putting our hopes and dreams and energy into those around us and not spending time getting to know our inner selves and finding ways to enjoy life independently, our pain most likely will be deeper and longer.

Loss and grief happens. Our friends, family and surroundings certainly help shape us and help us grow. Our constant companion is our self. It is important to love that self, so when life throws punches and loss happens, we will be better equipped to take on the challenges and work through them. This book has been a compilation of ideas to hopefully help you become better acquainted with yourself and to find ways to strengthen that inner love. Below are ways to incorporate your senses into self-care when grief has impacted your life.

Physical Exercise: Exercise often gets put on the back burner, forgotten or just simply the lack of motivation makes it seem impossible to fit into a daily routine. But, a workout actually helps shift one's mood. Exercise produces a "feel good" response and releases pent up energy. When we are avoiding it the most is when our body most likely needs it the most.

Consider a walk around the block, in nature or anywhere you can walk (at least 20 minutes), or try jogging, yoga, golf, Tai Qi, kickboxing, swimming, biking, surfing. Even just "shaking it out," which simply means standing up and shaking around, moving arms and feet (almost like what football players do in practice when they are just in place moving their arms and feet) can be a very effective way to relieve anxiety and release pent up energy.

Sleep: Sleep plays a very important role in our overall health. During restful sleep, a number of important factors are taking place. Cells are repairing themselves, the brain is recharging, the body releases important hormones, the immune system is boosted, and the cardiovascular system is given a chance to rest and recuperate. On the other hand, if one is not getting sufficient sleep, which has been noted to be at least seven to eight hours a night, the side effects of sleep deprivation can be quite debilitating over time. These include irritability, decreased cognitive ability, longer reaction time, and over longer periods of time can include mental distress, anxiety, depression and other emotional disorders. (Harding, 2015). So, getting good sleep is a vital part of the whole healing. Without sleep, it is difficult to function in the most basic daily tasks, much less work through grief.

The National Sleep Foundation has provided a variety of tips to help one get better rest. Tips include dimming lights, having a relaxed, peaceful room, keeping the room cool, having a comfortable bed, reducing noises, surrounding self with scents you like, and no caffeine or exercise late in the day as both are stimulating. If these adjustments aren't enough, I recommend a consultation with your primary physician to talk further about other short-term solutions to getting good sleep.

An interesting fact about dopamine, a neurotransmitter/chemical released in the brain that helps one feel good, is that levels increase when we are dreaming and also when we are awake being creative (Kluger, 2018).

Negative Ions (Mother Nature's Gift to Us): are created in nature as air molecules break apart due to sunlight radiation, ultraviolet rays, the vital energy of plants and moving air and water, and are not harmful even at higher levels, but to the contrary are quite beneficial to health and well being. It is believed that negative ions are actually biologically active and make a positive impact on the natural 24-hour cycle. Exposure to negative ions reduces stress and enhances overall performance as it increases blood and oxygen flow to the brain. Also, the negative ions provide a boost of the neurotransmitter serotonin, which literally creates the feeling of happiness (Phyto 5, 2018).

Places with a high concentration of negative ions are mountains, parks, waterfalls, fountains, bathroom shower, springs, beaches, pounding surf, forests, especially pine forests, moving air/wind, dirt/earth. There are ways to generate negative ions in your home by using indoor fountains, having plants, walking barefoot to be grounded to earth, and one of my favorite ways of exposure to negative ions within the home is the Himalayan Salt Lamp. Himalayan Salt Lamps provide color and light therapy with a warm and soft glow that is very calming for

Lamp

the anxious body/mind. It is a great night light, helping to provide more restful sleep, improves indoor air quality, and is soothing for people with allergies, among other benefits. (Phyto 5, 2018).

In our environment, we are exposed to positive ions and toxins in the air in a variety of places especially offices, factories and shopping malls. (Phyto 5, 2018). Therefore it is really important for mental health and well being to provide some nurturance and healing for our body by finding ways to be connected with nature on a daily basis.

Aromatherapy: by definition is the use of essential oils, which are oils derived from plant essences, and used for a therapeutic purpose. Science has proven that scents have a psychological impact on people. What do essential oils do? These plant essences are very concentrated in active molecules. They are known to lessen the effects of particular emotions such as depression and anxiety, and provide a sense of balance and well being. They work because aromatic essences have a direct path to the brain, more so than any other sensory system, suggests Dr. Garrison,

ND, in Kirkland, Washington. The aromas act on the brain's limbic system, the emotional center in the brain. "Essential oils can be the key to help unlock issues, whether these issues are at the surface or not," explained Dr. Garrison in Marian Smith's article from *Holistic Health News* (1999, para. 5), "It is thought that, by using essential oils for grief, one can balance the autonomic nervous activity of the body and the limbic center. That includes the state of mind, the heart rate and the blood pressure," suggests the *Essential Bazaar* article (2019, para.10). Within the realm of grief, one can feel just about any and every feeling, therefore, depending on the current need, there might be an essential oil to help support the process.

Essential Bazaar (2019, para. 13) mentions that there is one rule, though: "You must always pick the oils you like best. The best ones are those that don't evoke any bad memories when you inhale them. Even though some oils are more appropriate for certain situations, you should always go with the ones you like." In doing so, and using the right combination of essential oils, it can produce a feeling of calm and peace to allow one to do deeper inner work.

In Gabriel Mojay's book (1996) titled "Aromatherapy for Healing the Spirit," he shares that grief has an important and positive role to play in the process of both accepting and letting go of loss. Many of the below suggested oils help that process of transformation and letting go. Those grieving often get "stuck" and need help moving through the emotions and/or the tough times.

Cypress, frankincense and myrrh are suggested for someone stuck, unable to move forward; and facilitate change and transition. Eucalyptus opens the chest and encourages a more expansive sense of awareness. Clary Sage is used for one who is feeling melancholy, experiencing chronic tension and nervous strain; "It restores inner strength when we have overstretched ourselves."

Hyssop, Pine, Eucalyptus and Cypress lift feelings of negativity and foster letting go. Tea Tree Oil is used if the grief is impacting and weakening the immune system (Mojay, 1996, 174-177).

I also feel it is important to include Vetiver which calms the anxious mind and body. Lavender helps with restful sleep and provides overall calm. Bergamot is helpful for when someone is feeling sadness.

As with any sense, each person experiences essential oils in a different way based on past experiences and tolerances for different smells. So, while research shows that the above oils help with various ailments, it is important to listen to yourself and know that what works for one does not necessarily work for another. With most things in life, it is a trial and error experience. If essential oil doesn't work, try something else.*

Nutrition: The Chinese philosophy is about creating balance with a variety of whole foods. The specifics of diet are individual, based on constitution, illnesses, and seasons of the year. Chinese Medicine uses the tongue and pulses on the wrists to evaluate the constitution and determine the most appropriate food choices to create balance in the individual. The

> "Chinese Medicine View into Healing" by Cathy McNease, Dipl. of Chinese Herbology

human body/mind is seen as a mini version of the external world with patterns and associations, weaknesses and strengths, excesses and deficiencies.

Grief affects all of our organs, but most specifically the lung organ system, often causing a cough, wheezing and shortness of breath. Herbs may be used to help move grief out of the lungs. When loss comes as a shock, the kidney (and adrenal) organ system is profoundly affected, and may lead to a recurrence of that bolt of shock that initially came with the loss, like a kind of traumatic flashback. No matter which organs are impacted by the loss, a nutrient rich diet with colorful vegetables and fruits, lean proteins, whole grains, beans, nuts and seeds, while minimizing sugar and processed foods, will provide support.

The following chart shows some of the associations observed in Chinese Medicine, including the emotions. Emotions are intended to be helpers, but when they are either too extreme or long-standing, than illnesses can be triggered.

*I, personally, have found a lot of healing through various essential oils offered by doTERRA® What is unique about doTERRA® is that they make a high quality product in which many of their essential oils can be used internally for a deeper healing for both emotional and physical well being.

There is a connection between strong emotions and the immune system function, often weakened by emotional stress. The chart shows the five elements found in nature and the corresponding organs and senses. So for example, the Wood element is associated with the Liver/Gall Bladder and the emotions of anger, depression and frustration. An imbalance in the Liver can lead to those emotions and those emotions can be injurious to the Liver organ system. The color green is utilized to balance that condition by eating more green foods which will relax the Liver and thereby the anger. Also, it will help to visually surround oneself with the color Green, known to be a calming color. By applying the colors this way we can begin to restore balance to the person feeling angry.

ELEMENT	BODY ORGANS	SENSE ORGANS	EMOTIONS	COLOR
Wood	Liver/Gallbladder	Eyes/Vision	Anger/Depression/ Frustration	Green
Fire	Heart/Small Intestine	"Emotional heart"/ Feelings Tongue/ Talking	All emotions are felt by the Heart/ Over stimulation/ Excess Joy/Mania	Red
Earth	Spleen/Stomach Pancreas (digestive system)	Mouth/Tastes	Worry/ Over thinking	Yellow
Metal	Lungs/Large Intestines	Nose/Smells Skin/Touch	Sadness/Grief	White
Water	Kidneys/ Bladder Adrenals	Ears/Hearing	Fear/Anxiety/Shock	Black/ Dark Colors

Taking breaks, having fun, being in Nature. It is important to be kind to yourself and take time to slow down and breathe. Carving out space in your day to allow yourself to be in the present moment, the here and now, and what it has to offer.

Yoga at beach

Children really do this well and, if we allow ourselves the opportunity, we can learn from them. This ability to truly just be in the present moment. Not thinking about tomorrow or yesterday or even two hours from now, but just being in the NOW.

To fully immerse yourself in the NOW, the first step is to disconnect from the electronic world. If you live in a noisy area, invest in noise cancelling headphones and take a walk, if even just to your backyard. Stop to smell a flower, take a moment to look at the formation of clouds in the sky, study a piece of art, notice the texture of a leaf, really take in the colors surrounding you in a given moment, notice the effect of morning dew on spider webs, plants, and such, indulge in a sweet treat, or something savory if that is your tempo, put on a feel good song and dance. Learn how to meditate, create a mantra, explore, experiment, step outside the box and try something new, go camping. Just exercise the NOW, even if it's just for a brief moment in each day. Your heart and mind will thank you.

Dog running on beach. Photo Credit: Paul Dunkley

"The past is history, the future is a mystery, but the present, that is a gift." Very well-known phrase, and for good reason. As human beings, it is just our nature to get caught up in everything but the present moment. For anyone who has a cat or a dog, have you ever noticed that they are always just in the moment. We can learn a lot from them. Rediscover yourself, what lights you up, makes you giddy. It's inside you, instilled in you, and just needs to be nurtured and acknowledged. Give yourself permission to let go of it all and Just BE.

In closing, as I studied this most amazing photo captured by my dear friend Paul Dunkley, it demonstrates the juxtaposition of life and death, holding both and in all its glory and pain.

There is a lot we can learn about ourselves and ways we can grow through the impact of profound loss, but it takes time, patience, love for self, a good support system and some valuable tools.

My hope is that this book will enable you to be with your grief and move through it in a healthy and meaningful way on your healing journey.

Tree in night sky. Photo Credit: Paul Dunkley

Resources

Bilow, R. (May 14, 2014). When it comes to taste, what matters are: Our mouths or our minds? *bon appetit.* https://www.bonappetit.com/entertaining-style/trends-news/article/psychology-of-taste.

Bunkers, T. (2011). *The art journal workshop.* Beverly, MA: Quayside.

Color psychology: The emotional effects of colors. http://www.arttherapyblog.com/ (Copyright 2007-2019).

Fincher, J. (1985). The brain: Mystery of matter and mind. *The Human Body.* Washington DC: US News Books.

Frost, S. B. (2010). *SoulCollage® Evolving: An Intuitive Collage Process for Self-Discovery & Community.* Santa Cruz, CA: Hanford Mead.

Goldstein, B. (March 3, 2018). Music and the brain: The fascinating ways that music affects your mood and mind. *Conscious Lifestyle Magazine.* https://www.consciouslifestylemag.com/music-and-the-brain-affects-mood/

Gruson, L. (October 19, 1982). Color has a powerful effect on behavior, researchers assert. The *New York Times.* https://www.nytimes.com/1982/10/19/science/color-has-a-power-ful-effect-on-behavior-researchers-assert.html.

Harding, K. (2015). Importance of sleep. *Healthy lifestyles blog.* Salt Lake County.

Hoss, R. (2005). *Dream Language: Self-understanding through imagery and color.* Innersource publishing.

Kabat-Zinn, J. (Nov.1, 2007). Arriving at your own Door: 108 lessons in mindfulness. Hachette Books, 1 edition. https://www.goodreads.com/author/quotes/8750.Jon_Kabat_Zinn?page=3

Kluger, J. (2018). The power of sleep: Our uncensored, slumbering brains can dream up limitless vistas. The science of creativity. *Time Magazine.*

Malchiodi, C. (2007). *The art therapy sourcebook.*

Malchiodi, C. (2003). *Handbook of art therapy.* New York: Guilford.

Malchiodi, C. (2002). The soul's palette: Drawing on art's transformative powers for health and well-being.

Mandali, M. (1994). *Everyone's mandala coloring book. Vol. 2.* Helena, MT: Mandali.

McNamee, C. (2004). Using both sides of the brain: Experiences that integrate art and talk therapy through scribble drawings. *Art Therapy: Journal of the American Art Therapy Association. Mundelein,* IL: AATA, Inc. 2. (3), 136-142.

McNease, C. (2014). *In harmony with the seasons: Herbs, nutrition, and well-being.* New York: Made Mark.

Mojay, G. (1996). Aromatherapy for healing the spirit: A guide to restoring emotional and mental balance through essential oils. New York: Henry Holt.

Liebenow, M. (2018). The metabolism of grief. https://widowersgrief.blogspot.com.

Lokos, A. (Feb. 18, 2010). Pocket peace: Effective practices for enlightened living. Tarcherperigee publishing. https://www.goodreads.com/author/quotes/3335092.Allan_Lokos.

Newton, P & D (2000). Taste and smell. Public television's family science show. Newton's Apple. http://ericir.syr.edu/Projects/Newton/11/tstesmll.html.

Phillips, C. (2004). *Color for life*. New York: Ryland Peters & Small.

PHYTO 5 (2018). 8 ways to expose yourself to earth's healing negative ions. Eustis, FL: Phyto Distribution.

Perls, F. (2019) cited in https://www.azquotes.com/author/18137-Frederick_Salomon_Perls.

Perls, F. (2019) https://exploringyourmind.com/the-35-best-fritz-perls-quotes/

Psychology and smell. (2015). *Fifthsense*. www.fifthsense.org.uk/psychology-and-smell.

Ransom, M (2016). *Courage road: A guide from grief to hope*. Mary Ransom.

Salzberg, S. (2011). Real happiness: the power of meditation. Workman Publishing.

Shapiro, F. (1995). *Eye movement desensitization and reprocessing (EMDR) Therapy, 3rd Ed.* New York: Guilford.

Smith, M. (1999). Aromatherapy: A healing facilitator. *Holistic Health News*.

The beauty and wisdom of pure essential oils. www.essentialbazaar.com/best essential oils for grief. (2019).

Trout, D. (2009). *Journal spilling: Mixed-Media techniques for free expression*. Cincinnati, OH: North Light Books.

Van der Kolk, B. (1994). The body keeps the score: Memory and the evolving psychobiology of post traumatic stress. *Harvard Review of Psychiatry*. 1, (5), 253-265.

Sunset at the beach. Photo Credit: Harmony Moon Photography.

Valerie Moore-Altavilla, LCSW

Valerie is an Art Therapist, Soulcollage® Facilitator, and trained in EMDR. She instinctively used the expressive arts to metabolize grief from the multiple losses of her loved ones that began when she was 11. Now, professionally trained in the career for which life was already preparing her, she shares in *All You Need Is What You Have* what she has learned about how to grieve. Valerie trusts you to know which expressive exercise to start with and how to proceed on your healing journey from there. She guides you in taking stock of your strengths as well as your losses and how to make a comfort journal to soothe yourself. She shares easy projects that will help you move along the grieving path through all its memories, feelings, thoughts, and sensations. Valerie facilitates workshops and retreats and can be reached through her website at MooreHealingArtTherapy.com.